LETTING
GO
of LEGACY
SERVICES

ALA Editions purchases fund advocacy, awareness, and
accreditation programs for library professionals worldwide.

LETTING GO

of LEGACY SERVICES

Library Case Studies

Edited by Mary Evangeliste
and Katherine Furlong

ala
editions

An imprint of the American Library Association
CHICAGO 2014

Printed in the United States of America
18 17 16 15 14   5 4 3 2 1

Extensive effort has gone into ensuring the reliability of the information in this book; however, the publisher makes no warranty, express or implied, with respect to the material contained herein.

ISBN: 978-0-8389-1220-1 (paper).

Library of Congress Cataloging-in-Publication Data

Letting go of legacy services : library case studies / [edited by] Mary Evangeliste and
    Katherine Furlong.
  pages   cm
Includes bibliographical references and index.
ISBN 978-0-8389-1220-1 (softcover : alk. paper)
    1. Library administration—United States—Case studies. 2. Library planning—
    United States—Case studies. 3. Libraries—United States—Reorganization—
    Case studies. 4. Public services (Libraries)—United States—Case studies.
    5. Organizational change—United States—Case studies. 6. Organizational
    effectiveness—United States—Case studies. I. Evangeliste, Mary, editor of
    compilation. II. Furlong, Katherine, editor of compilation.
Z678.L43 2014
025.1—dc23   2014000998

♾ This paper meets the requirements of ANSI/NISO Z39.48-1992
(Permanence of Paper).

Contents

Acknowledgments vii

Introduction ix

1 | **Lafayette College** 1

Cutting Costs, Increasing Access: Pay-Per-View Periodicals
at Lafayette College Libraries *2*

Bookend *6*

Interview: David Consiglio *8*

2 | **Cumberland County Library System** 13

Moving to Web-Based Services: How Smart Planning
and Staff Training Factored into a Complete Website
Overhaul—and Improved Community Outreach *14*

Bookend *28*

3 | **University of Arizona Libraries** 29

Being Relevant in the 21st Century: Elimination of Physical
and Electronic Reserve Services *30*

Bookend *41*

4 | **Oregon State University** 43

Magical Thinking: Moving Beyond Natural Bias
to Examine Core Services *44*

Bookend *57*

5 | **University of California, Santa Cruz** 59

A Good Crisis: Reinventing Critical Services *60*

Bookend *72*

6 | **University of North Carolina at Charlotte** 73

A New Way to Think: Anthropological Research
Uncovers Powerful Ideas *74*

Bookend *85*

7 | **American University** 87

A Focus on Buy-in: Facilitating the Shift to Electronic
Resources through Collaborative Strategic Planning *88*

Bookend *102*

Interview: Valerie Diggs *104*

8 | **Rosenberg Library** 111

After Ike: Evaluating Long-Held Practices under Scrutiny *112*

Bookend *119*

9 | **University of West Florida** 121

The Great Good Place: Creating Space
for Knowledge Creation *122*

Bookend *130*

Conclusion 133

About the Authors and Contributors 143

Bibliography 147

Index 153

Acknowledgments

The authors would like to thank Sue Alman for her graciousness of spirit and professional inspiration. We love you, Sue!

Mary's acknowledgments

I would like to thank all of those who mentored me in my library career: Helen Goldstein, Diana Vogelsong

I would like to thank my coeditor Katherine Furlong for her tenacity and creativity and fearlessness

And to my colleagues, who constantly inform, challenge, and expand my ideas of librarianship: Cody Aune, Karen Downing, Tara Fox-Lupo, Brenna Haebel, Alex Hodges, Yvonne Mery, Alex Rivera, Gwendolyn Reece and Katherine Simpson

And to my most cherished creative partner, Jonathan Silberman

Katherine's acknowledgments

Dean Neil McElroy and my colleagues at Skillman Library, who allowed me to be "invisible" for the summer of 2012

Provost Wendy Hill and Lafayette College for granting my professional development leave

Nina Gilbert, editor extraordinaire

Ann Furlong, for many things, including introducing me to Frances Hesselbein's book

My Frye cohorts, especially Amy, Dave, Gentry and Julie

Mary Evangeliste, for believing we could do it, and for making me laugh in the darkest of days

Scott, David, and Genevieve, for their unfailing love and support

Introduction

Ice Cream

IT ALL BEGAN, as many good things do, with ice cream. The authors met while attending an ice cream social at a library consortium event at Penn State University. We bonded over our mutual love of creamery goodness, and began to talk about new technologies, allocating budgets, management, and decision making in our respective liberal arts colleges. It didn't take long to realize that our issues were shared, and that our struggles might be easier if we pooled resources. While we were discussing the need to stop doing things that seemed redundant or counterintuitive, we made the intuitive choice to sit down and have a second helping of ice cream. We started comparing notes on services, priorities, and management philosophies, quickly realizing that working at very similar institutions would give us the opportunity to share information and evidence gathering techniques as we critically examined services in our individual libraries. Our campus and library cultures were somewhat different, but we recognized that our similarities meant we could work together to make the process easier. In our initial conversations, we may not have been using the words "planned abandonment" or even have thought about a framework for decision making, but over time, we quickly discovered that an ideal of organized, systematic analysis of service was an important tool when contemplating innovative change in our organizations. So when we returned to our own institutions we started to read, think, and gather evidence.

While ice cream may have brought us together, our shared western Pennsylvania roots and our history in the Girl Scouts brought us to read Frances Hesselbein on management. Hesselbein, a native of Katherine's hometown of Johnstown, Pennsylvania, was the CEO of the Girl Scouts of America and a protégée of Peter Drucker. In her writings she challenges leaders to identify and discard what no longer works to ensure that services and organizations are relevant for the future. Hesselbein credits the concept of planned abandonment to Peter Drucker, and reading Drucker gave us a framework to more fully understand the theory of planned abandonment.

Planned Abandonment

Planned abandonment means examining and possibly ending the services that brought a library success in the past and, instead, continually establishing new means of being relevant to our patrons and communities. Those of us who have worked in libraries for any length of time know that as a breed, library workers often propose and add new services, but don't always critically examine existing realities in light of our missions, and rarely let go of obsolete or less useful programs. It's terribly difficult, if not impossible, to innovate in big or important ways if you also have to keep doing everything you've always done. In a 2003 interview, Drucker stressed that innovation isn't "something one can add to a static organization." He went on to state that the "first requirement" of being an innovative organization is to embrace "organized systematic abandonment."[1] Drucker and Hesselbein agree on the need for examination, for action, for addressing "what we do now" if services or products no longer make sense. While the subject of planned abandonment might have particular relevance during an economic downturn, examining services should be a regular part of organizational assessment and decision making.

Let's get one thing clear at the beginning of this book. We're not arguing that librarians don't change. We know for a fact that we do—we're innovating and changing all the time. The library world has been revolutionized several times over in the past few decades. Librarians are really, really good at change. But we aren't always good at valuing what we do, and we don't always manage change in a way that mitigates the possibility of a Nicholson Baker-type blowback.

This also isn't a book full of management techniques. Librarians are rightly skeptical of delving too far into the business and management literature for inspiration. Following every trendy management idea is a bad idea for businesses, let alone libraries. We're not going to move your cheese, or compel you to fling fish or annoy you with acronyms. There are no Sigmas here. We are going to challenge you to accept that at the core of Drucker's ideas about abandonment are concepts that librarians hold dear: critical thinking, analysis, and assessment. Questioning our beliefs, our practices, and the things we've held sacred is healthy and necessary in order to reflect on what we value and the future of our profession. Letting go of things that no longer bring value to your organization is also a sane and compassionate response to a profession that needs to be able to respond to change with wisdom. We cannot do it all, nor should we try.

Jack Welch of GE famously used Drucker's planned abandonment strategies when he took over the company. After asking the question "if you were not already in this business, would you enter it today, knowing what you know?" Welch sold off GE's small appliance division and then, after that proved to be a correct move, sold off the consumer electronics division a few years later. Welch argued that freeing up the resources that had been invested in these legacy products allowed GE to focus on its strengths (high-technology business, like medical equipment and airplane parts) and core services such as lighting.

Drucker himself used General Motors as an example of a company that failed to use planned abandonment concepts when it created the Saturn automobile line. Saturn's assembly line worker participation culture and unique customer service focus were departures from staid Detroit industry standards. Initially the car line was a success, but GM failed to abandon its old lines such as Oldsmobile and truly commit to the radically different Saturn practices. As a result, too few resources were devoted to too many GM product lines—and the last Saturn rolled off the assembly lines in 2009.

For another example, some Girl Scout Councils used planned abandonment strategies in 2011 to discover that the top five varieties of Girl Scout cookies make up 77 percent of cookie sales, and cut other cookie lines accordingly. The so-called "Super Six pilot program" was a teachable moment for the organization, and an opportunity to see if a streamlined product line, combined with increased training, resulted in operating efficiencies, increased sales, and customer satisfaction. So if you miss the Dulce de Leche cookie, you can blame planned abandonment strategies for its absence.

Unfortunately, human nature works against planned abandonment principles. We like doing what we know, and when you're in the midst of fulfilling work, and hearing feedback from enthusiastic supporters, it is difficult to understand the need for change. As the Girl Scouts learned, some people really like underperforming cookies, and have a hard time letting go. Librarians recognize that ending services can be especially hard. Stoffle, Leeder, and Sykes-Casavant state in their article, "Bridging the Gap: Wherever you are, the Library," "This is a difficult challenge for librarians, as we typically hesitate to end a service even if there is one person in our entire community who uses it."[2]

This is where planned abandonment can help.

Through the use of planned abandonment strategies grounded in assessment-based decision making, our organizations can consciously focus on what we can and must do well, and start the process of choosing what services to let go. This book's case studies and interviews reveal that the process must be context-sensitive and requires careful communication and follow-through from all levels of library management. Of course, federal, state, and local laws, as well as institutional policies, have to be kept in mind when evaluating services—but services must be evaluated.

And So . . .

Once we understood the concept of planned abandonment, we decided to put the theory into practice in our own libraries. We conducted a literature review, and found that while libraries might be abandoning things, very few libraries were using the term "planned abandonment." While as far back as 1994, articles mention Drucker's ideas and their possible application to libraries, we found no case studies on the abandonment of a legacy service. So we decided to create our own in-house study of interlibrary loan practices. We worked together, framed questions, analyzed data, and ultimately decided to end a once-popular interlibrary borrowing program. The resulting paper was presented at an ACRL conference in 2011, and sparked interest and debate.[3]

Librarians embraced the overarching principles of planned abandonment. We've presented online and at conferences, and the more we interacted with colleagues, the more we learned about the many reasons why librarians do not adopt planned abandonment. Most of these reasons are based on assumptions, emotional responses, and a general discomfort with getting rid of anything. One academic librarian who writes on these issues is Donald Gilstrap, dean of University Libraries at Wichita State. Gilstrap proposes that although maintaining old and new ways of doing things may allow libraries to avoid facing the anxiety of "endings," not adopting planned abandonment may heighten these anxieties by not allowing the librarians to create "new beginnings" with less confusion and not as much stress from maintaining too many services and systems.[4]

Librarians are often comfortable with adding new services but are much less comfortable with taking anything away. But Gilstrap's study seems at odds with the fact that as a profession we have radically adapted the way library services are accessed and delivered over the past twenty years.

Why Case Studies?

Once we stepped back and looked at what we had already accomplished, we realized that choosing to work together as we developed our questions, collected our data, and framed our solutions was the most important support in analyzing our own libraries' services and practices. Working together helped us to reach conclusions faster than if we were working alone. This is why we then decided to reach out to others in writing this book, and ask for experienced librarians at a variety of libraries to write case studies as a means to explore the broader topic of how we can face the future.

We chose to use case studies because they are an effective tool for deep thought and analysis, offering a real-life glimpse of how one library dealt with a difficult issue. Through the careful analysis of case studies, readers can gain insight into how their colleagues have grappled with choices to abandon—or in some cases, to keep and alter services. We asked the authors of the studies to be candid, to share their data analysis techniques and their decision-making frameworks.

These case studies are not prescriptive; they are lenses through which we can examine a service and to illustrate trends and decision-making methods. You won't be able to copy an approach because your situation, management structure, budget, and personnel will vary greatly from those in the case studies. But each case study will show how librarians grounded their decision making in their own institutional values and provide insight and inspiration to you as you grapple with your own challenges.

Why Interviews?

As we were reviewing the case studies and studying the concepts of planned abandonment, we quickly identified pressure points common across many different libraries. These pressure points included difficulties in dealing with data, in communicating to internal and external populations, and in the constant stress of just working together in organizations. We interviewed librarians to find commonsense solutions for dealing with these issues.

Let's Go

This book is not telling you that you have to change. This book provides an approach to something that will never go away: the future. Through examining the case studies and carefully reading the interviews, you can develop a framework to start to think about what is vitally important for your library's future. You will discover ways to identify services, activities, and practices that can be let go, freeing you to focus on valuable, mission-critical work.

Just remember: It's all easier with ice cream and friends.

REFERENCES

1. Shaker A. Zahra, "An Interview with Peter Drucker," *The Academy of Management Executive* 17, no. 3 (2003): 11.

2. Carla J. Stoffle, Kim Leeder, and Gabrielle Sykes-Casavant, "Bridging the Gap: Wherever you are, the Library," *Journal of Library Administration* 48, no. 1 (2008): 19.

3. Mary Evangeliste and Katherine Furlong, "When Interdependence Becomes Co-dependence: Knowing When and How to Let Go of Legacy Services" in Declaration of Interdependence: The Proceedings of the ACRL 2011 Conference, March 30–April 2, 2011, Philadelphia, PA., 2011.

4. Donald L. Gilstrap, "Librarians and the Complexity of Individual and Organizational Change: Case Study Findings of an Emergent Research Library," *Advances in Library Administration and Organization* 28 (2009): 1–58.

Case Study 1 | # Lafayette College

SOMETIMES WE GET so emotionally attached to a service or an idea that sheer nostalgia makes it difficult to abandon it for something new. This is when the Adrien Brody Rule can come into play. You see, Adrien Brody was to be the star of the Terrence Malick film *The Thin Red Line*. Brody's character is the main protagonist in the source material, a novel by James Jones. Brody endured boot camp and spent six months of his life filming under grueling conditions, with every impression that he was the star of the show. And then the editing began. As the director shaped the film, more and more of Brody's character ended up on the cutting room floor, until his lead role as Corporal Fife morphed into a minor supporting character.

According to an editorial in *Fast Company* magazine, the point of the Adrien Brody Rule is that "you can't make decisions based on initial assumptions or the amount of resources extended, but solely on what best meets the needs of the situation."[1] Terrence Malick's telling of *The Thin Red Line* didn't need Adrien Brody. Adrien Brody might have been cast as the star, worked very hard at his role, but in the end he wasn't really needed. Librarians at Lafayette College put the Adrien Brody Rule into practice when they evaluated their periodical subscriptions. They discovered that their historical reliance on print periodical subscriptions and a faculty-based selection process was no longer the best way to meet the needs of their community. The journals hit the cutting room floor, and pay-per-view access became the star.

Cutting Costs, Increasing Access

Pay-Per-View Periodicals at Lafayette College Libraries

Michael Hanson and Terese Heidenwolf

LAFAYETTE COLLEGE, AN undergraduate private liberal arts and engineering school in Easton, Pennsylvania, serves a population of 2,400 students and 200 faculty members. With a strong curricular emphasis on science and engineering, Lafayette libraries have traditionally spent heavily in STEM periodical titles.

Lafayette libraries' strategy for providing users with access to serials underwent an important modification in 2008, when we cut subscriptions to all of our Elsevier journals and switched to pay-per-view access. For the previous decade we had been struggling with the challenges presented by the migration of serials literature from print to electronic format coupled with the inflation of serials prices and stagnant library budgets. As serials costs inflated, we were twice required to implement a series of cuts, during which departments were asked to reduce their subscription list by a certain dollar amount. Despite the necessity of cuts, faculty continued to request new journal subscriptions, particularly costly STEM titles. Elsevier published some of the most requested titles, but because of the amount we were already spending on subscriptions to Elsevier journals, the publisher was unwilling to offer us their "small school discount" to the suite of journals in ScienceDirect.

With this option closed to us and with a stagnant budget making more serials cuts imminent, we began to explore pay-per-view options, which seemed to offer a way to provide users with access to more of the content they were asking for. We couldn't afford to maintain our print subscriptions while also offering pay-per-view access to non-subscribed titles, so we began to consider cutting subscriptions to all of our Elsevier serials. While there was little doubt that faculty and students would be pleased by increased access provided via pay-per-view, we were concerned that the logistics might be a stumbling block for users, that the costs would be unpredictable, and that we would no longer be building a permanent archive of journals, either in print or electronically.

Although the unpredictability of the costs at first seemed disconcerting, when we started doing calculations, we quickly realized that it was reasonable to assume that the money saved by canceling Elsevier subscriptions would more than cover pay-per-view demand for a year. With a fee of $30 per article, our user population of 200 faculty and 2,400 students would have to access well over 5,000 articles in a year to exceed what we were spending on Elsevier subscriptions. We still felt a bit queasy knowing that we would no longer be purchasing permanent access to these journals, but consoled ourselves with the thought that given the ready availability of electronic archives, we could purchase permanent access to some titles down the line if pay-per-view stopped meeting our needs.

So, in early 2008, we tested the waters by conducting a trial for faculty in biology and geology. For one semester we provided them with immediate, unlimited access to nearly all of Elsevier's titles, with the library paying the entire bill. When we saw that the trial had gone smoothly, we began talking with faculty about canceling our Elsevier subscriptions and relying entirely on pay-per-view access. After getting preliminary endorsement from the Library Advisory Committee, which consisted of three faculty members and two students, we held a meeting with faculty collection coordinators, where we presented them with our plan and provided a list of the titles that would be cut. Although a few of them were initially concerned about the high cost per article, they were quickly convinced that it was reasonable given how much we were already paying for a small number of subscriptions, and they expressed no other reservations.

We were then left to work out the logistics of providing access. After consulting with colleagues at a few similar institutions that had migrated to pay-per-view, we decided to provide all faculty with unlimited, unmediated access through our established OpenURL link resolver, rather than allocating certain pools of money for individual departments to spend. Faculty enjoy convenient click-through access to article PDFs. To control the costs of the program, student access was mediated via an online interface that forwarded an e-mail request to a staff member. The staff member would either e-mail the requested article to the student (within two hours during regular reference hours) or, if the article was available in the print collection, direct the student to the paper copy. This modest requesting "hurdle" increased the probability that a student genuinely wanted the article and decreased the casual downloading that could inflate the cost of the program. Information about each title available was included in the library catalog and coverage information was added to our OpenURL resolver's knowledge base.

By January 2009, all of our policies and procedures were in place, and faculty and students were able to access nearly all articles available from Elsevier. We posted news of the change on our website and informed faculty via an e-mail message and an article in the library newsletter. We did no special promotion to students, but they quickly discovered the availability of the materials when they used our databases and OpenURL resolver.

Simultaneously we cancelled 77 Elsevier subscriptions, for which we had been paying $162,662. (The following year, we cancelled our twenty-one Elsevier standing orders.) In that first year of pay-per-view, faculty and students accessed 2,147 articles at a newly negotiated price of $22 each for a total cost of $47,234. It would be nice to say that with the savings of over $115,000 we were able to purchase additional materials, but in fact, this savings merely allowed us to keep our serials budget balanced and gave us some breathing room for the coming year, when our budget allocations were fairly stagnant. It is not insignificant that our interlibrary loan use statistics and costs were decreasing in lockstep with our pay-per-view access.

The increased access to Elsevier titles was so appreciated by our users and was so easy for us to manage, that the following year we implemented pay-per-view for Wiley articles and will likely make the change with additional publishers. The increased Wiley access was greeted with nearly as much enthusiasm as the Elsevier access had been, and we received many notes of thanks from faculty, including one exuberant (if slightly alarming) message that read, "Woo hoo!!!! Picture me lighting my hair on fire and running around my office right now!"

With the implementation of pay-per-view access, we also saw an opportunity to evaluate our serials selection and review processes, which unexpectedly led to another modification in our practices. For many years, in order to collect serials materials that best fit faculty and student needs, each academic department reviewed a list of current subscriptions in support of their discipline. If faculty felt the titles didn't meet their needs, they then could request different or additional titles, which the library tried to accommodate within the limits of our budget and competing requests. Since faculty were reviewing serials lists annually and had recently been forced to winnow them, we had felt fairly confident that the titles we subscribed to were of high importance to our faculty's research and instruction and, by extension, to their students' needs. Now that our faculty and students had access to nearly all Elsevier titles, we could collect use data to test this assumption. After a year of this program, an examination of the data showed that the subscription lists were not accurate predictors of the journals faculty and students used when given access to the full complement of Elsevier titles, and we began to reevaluate the primacy that we had given to faculty opinions in the serials selection process.

Library literature is replete with examinations comparing patron-driven selection to collection developers' selections. Most conclude that selectors' choices do not predict users' choices and that broad access, generally satisfied by publisher Big Deal packages, best meets user demand. Considering these studies, perhaps we shouldn't have been surprised that our selected titles didn't better match those with high pay-per-view use. We had thought that giving faculty voices priority in the selection process as well as monitoring interlibrary loan requests created a process that captured some nuances that might have made our selection results more useful for our user community.

When we examined data from 2009, our first year of Elsevier pay-per-view access, we found that articles from twenty-seven titles were downloaded more than ten times and accounted for nearly 30 percent of all use. Of these, eight had been on our subscription list, three we had considered subscribing to, and four were at least familiar because they were requested fairly frequently via interlibrary loan. But twelve of these high-use titles weren't even on our radar screen. We had had no faculty requests to purchase them in recent years and none of them were requested more than ten times via interlibrary loan in 2008. (In fact, most had fewer than five requests.)

We continued to monitor our use data and noticed patterns from year to year. In 2009, for example, 32 of the 98 titles we had previously subscribed to were not used at all; in 2011, 43 of these 98 titles were not used. In more than three years of pay-per-view access, 21 of the 98 titles we had subscribed to were never used, even when we took into account those requests for which we referred students to paper copies in our collection.

It is reasonable to assume that subscription selections would have shifted some since 2008 to meet new information demands. Still, the data do suggest that we gave the faculty more credit than we should have for being able to predict which journals would meet their needs. Perhaps the information environment is now so extensive and patrons' needs so diffuse, even among a user population as small as ours, that such predictions are nearly futile.

We still have individual subscriptions to thousands of periodicals and still consult annually with faculty about these subscription lists, but given the lessons we learned from our Elsevier data, we are now much more likely to let use data drive our decisions about which titles to retain and which to cut. Use statistics accompany the review lists sent to each department, and titles that have low use are highlighted with a request for the department to discuss their usefulness and consider replacing them with other titles. Titles that show low use over an extended period of time are cut by the library even if faculty have not identified them for cancellation.

Fortunately, unpredictability in the titles used via pay-per-view doesn't translate into unpredictable budget patterns. Over our several years of experience, overall demand has remained fairly stable from year to year and follows a pattern tied to the academic year. When classes are in session, student use is higher than faculty use and peaks during mid-semester and in the weeks just before the end of the semester. Faculty use increases when teaching loads are light, mostly in the summer months and during breaks, and then abates at the same times student use increases.

> Perhaps the information environment is so extensive and patrons' needs so diffuse, even among a user population as small as ours, that such predictions are nearly futile.

Although we are acutely aware that we are forsaking traditional library practice by not having a paper or licensed archival copy of Elsevier and Wiley journals, we think that the benefits realized in providing readier, wider, and cheaper access to these scholarly journals merit forsaking this practice. Abandoning so many of our serials subscriptions felt a bit like jumping off a cliff, but we're glad that we took the plunge—and our users are as well.

Bookend

LAFAYETTE'S CASE STUDY is a clear example of the Adrien Brody Rule in action. They made decisions based on what best met the needs of their current situation, casting aside nostalgia and historic investments in print collections. This is clearly an example that won't work for all types of libraries; research libraries with a preservation mandate might find the prospect impossible, impractical, and downright wrong. Nevertheless, the model of decision making based on values, patron service, cost, and use patterns is exactly the kind of thing all libraries can emulate. Abandoning nostalgia and critically examining past practice allowed librarians at Lafayette to rely more on data-driven decision making and planned abandonment practices.

Librarians in the profession long enough to remember Nicholson Baker realize that communication and planning are the keys to making something like Lafayette's pay-per-view service work. In his 2001 book *Double Fold: Libraries and the Assault on Paper,* Nicholson Baker accused librarians of destroying our common cultural heritage by discarding original journals and other materials after microfilming them, and characterized microformats as cumbersome barriers to scholarship and research. Baker's writings about library and archival practices ignited a firestorm in the profession. As Richard Cox, author of *Vandals in the Stacks? A Response to Nicholson Baker's Assault on Libraries,* stated, "Perhaps it will take such a rant from outside of our community to wake us up about what and how we need to communicate."[2]

Lafayette succeeded in their plan because they consulted stakeholders and clearly communicated the process, rationale, and benefits of the changed service along the way.

REFERENCES

1. Robert Safian, "Letter from the Editor: The Adrien Brody Rule," *Fast Company,* January 9, 2012, accessed May 10, 2012, www.fastcompany.com/1802659/letter-editor-adrien-brody-rule.

2. Richard J. Cox, *Vandals in the Stacks? A Response to Nicholson Baker's Assault on Libraries* (Westport, CT, Greenwood Press, 2002), 196.

The Data-Driven Approach to Library Management

An Interview with David Consiglio

Katherine Furlong

DAVID CONSIGLIO IS Head of Research Support and Educational Technology at Bryn Mawr College. Dave works with researchers and students in the areas of statistical, research and survey methodology. While pursuing his graduate degrees, Dave taught statistics, statistical programming, and research methodology at the University of Maryland. In 1996, he was hired by the University of Maryland to provide statistical, survey, and research methodology support for the Behavioral and Social Science faculty at the university. In 2001, Dave moved to Bryn Mawr College where he continues to work with faculty and students in these areas. Over the years he has developed and consulted on hundreds of surveys and research projects, including the MISO Survey of libraries and IT organizations. Dave's passion for libraries, research, and data makes his a unique voice in analytical, data-driven approaches to library management. Katherine Furlong interviewed Dave in December of 2012.

Katherine: Can you speak to the importance of data-driven decision making in libraries?

Dave: Let's step back. How are you defining data?

Katherine: Data can be quantitative (numbers), qualitative (observations); it can be any source of information you use in an evaluation of a service.

Dave: So you're using data broadly. It's important to define that. I think that when you combine quantitative data with qualitative data, you have your richest form of information. It is the single best guide when you make decisions for ninety percent of the day-to-day operations of a library or IT organization. Quantitative data on its own lacks context. Qualitative data on its own lacks generalizability. Combining quantitative and qualitative together is your richest form of data and richest form of information. I'm treating all my answers in the context of those two things put together, because I think it's absolutely critical that they be put together. Even though I'm a survey guy, I'm about using better information.

Katherine: So why is it important to use data-driven decision making to get better information?

Dave: Many reasons. Let's start from the experiential data that people have already collected versus the objective collection of data. Most of the time, people have a pretty good sense of the phenomena that are happening around them, particularly if they are doing anything on the ground with the work in the library. Ninety to ninety-five percent of the time, or greater, their instincts about what's happening in the library are dead-on accurate. So that's anecdotal, what your instincts and senses are telling you. Data-driven decisions, however, have a couple of advantages. First, they can confirm the anecdotal experience of the person. And like I said, about ninety-five percent of the time, that's what happens; it confirms your experience. But in that other five to ten percent of the time, the data can actually surprise you. And when the data surprises you, it has an interesting effect. It challenges your assumptions in regard to what you know. And if you care at a deeper level than just what the numbers say, and if you're a good researcher, you'll explore why the numbers don't meet up with what your gut said. Exploring that difference produces new knowledge. It's not the data that produces new knowledge: it's the exploration of the data.

The other reason data-driven decisions are so important is political. From a political perspective, you may very accurately know ninety-five percent of the phenomena that's happening around you. But when you need to speak up within your institution to those at a higher level, or outward, to an audience that's not used to doing the same thing you are, your anecdotal experience is just that—anecdotal. If you can match data and the narrative together, it creates a powerful political argument. It allows you to present objective measures in a context of subjective experiences.

Katherine: What are the problems or patterns you see in the way librarians use data?

Dave: Let me start with the other extreme. Making decisions solely based on data can be as improper as making decisions without any data at all. Data provides us additional information that we don't have otherwise, but we shouldn't ignore the other forms of data that we collect. If we make only data-driven decisions without trying to put that data in a greater context, then you're going to find yourself in a position where you may not make as many mistakes, but it also removes any risk taking. It can blind you to potential.

Katherine: Are you getting at serendipity or something like that?

Dave: A bit of serendipity, but actually, you're erasing the value of human intellect if you just assert, "this is what the numbers say" and leave it at that. Sometimes, it makes sense to say "those numbers in the context of other things that I know, other narratives, suggest to me that the right way forward is to do this thing." Numbers can show you a trend in a certain direction, but you might have good reason to do something else, because of your own intellect and experience.

I can give a good example of how the data can fail you. A few years ago, we saw these huge increases in the use of instant messaging (IM) among undergraduate students. Because the data was driving us toward "this is the way they're communicating," it would be very easy for us to conclude "using IM as the sole means of communication is good. This is where students are and will be." Now someone who is forward thinking might have noticed at a critical point about five years ago that there was a huge uptick in SMS text messaging. That might make you think that maybe you shouldn't sink a ton of resources into IM because text messaging might replace IM. Which is exactly what did happen. A purely data-driven decision would have pushed toward a huge, and faulty, IM investment. The data only captures the past and the present, but data can't see the future. You have to divine the future from what you see in the data and in your own experiences.

Katherine: So, back to problems in using data … all kinds of data …

Dave: There is generally a large-scale lack of sophistication when it comes to understanding both qualitative and quantitative data. And sometimes that lack of sophistication can lead to improper decisions, particularly if you combine a lack of sophistication with not using your human intelligence. That's when you run into problems.

I'm going to give a hypothetical example completely out of the library context. Let's say you're in a city. The sections of the city with the most churches also seem to have the highest rates of violence. So, because of that data, you decide that you must do something about the churches.

Now, it's an extreme example. It seems obvious that the churches are not causing the violence. A purely data-driven decision looks at this correlation versus causation issue. There's a correlation between churches and violence, but it's not a causal relationship. The causal relationship is that those portions of the city with more churches also have a higher density of population, and therefore, because of the higher density of population, you have more violence because there are more people around.

So, misunderstanding the nature of data and how to interpret it, particularly when you remove human intelligence and experience, can lead to bad conclusions that lead to bad decisions.

Now the third issue is the opposite of data-driven decisions, and it comes from ignorance. People who make data-driven decisions and make a mistake, and get burned by the decisions, can suffer from a recoil effect. It's throwing out the baby with the bathwater. I've seen this happen, where someone follows the numbers, makes a decision, is wrong, and therefore decides to never follow the numbers again.

Data can only give you part of the picture. You still need to use your brain.

Katherine: That's what's great about librarians. We use our brains, and encourage others to do the same.

Dave: This is probably obvious, but in this current environment in libraries, where resources are tighter, and expectations are changing all the time, libraries cannot afford to make as many mistakes. You are never going to be one hundred percent accurate in the decisions you make. You're also never going to be one hundred percent wrong in the decisions you make. But the pressures are on now for libraries to raise the percentage, to be closer to one hundred percent right. Because of that, it's important to take in all forms of information, of data, to make decisions. Simply put, we can't afford to make bad decisions.

Katherine: What advice do you have for those not comfortable with numbers and data analysis?

Dave: Ask for help. The good news is that I'm seeing the level of sophistication with numbers is rising. It's not where it needs to be, but it's rising because of the drive for assessment. People are realizing they need greater knowledge and better tools, and they're learning. They're starting to know what they don't know a bit more, and are more willing to turn to people who have some level of expertise.

Katherine: Do you have anything else to share?

Dave: I really do think there is a beautiful marriage between qualitative and quantitative data that needs to be used more by librarians in general. Too much of a reliance on one or the other gives a researcher an incomplete picture of what's going on in an organization. A commonly held view is that quantitative and qualitative analyses are at odds with one another. That's wrong. The qualitative data gives you stories, narratives, which feed into the quantitative measures. The quantitative data gives you an understanding of how generalized these narratives might be, and feed back into more qualitative research into the anomalies, the things you don't expect. Quantitative data is terrific for telling you what; it's terrible at telling you why. Qualitative data is terrific at telling you why, but does a terrible job of explaining the extent of an issue. The best research plays off both kinds of data in a beautiful, iterative, cyclical fashion.

Case Study 2 | # Cumberland County Library System

IN THE INTRODUCTION to this book, we discussed how, in 2011, some Girl Scout Councils had practiced planned abandonment by limiting the variety of cookies sold in their annual fund raiser and focusing only on the "high-performing" stock. Thin Mints were in, Dulce de Leches were decidedly out.

Fast forward one year, and a Time.com article describes how Scouts are now using social media and ever-present mobile devices to shatter cookie sales records. By exploiting every technical tool at their disposal, the Girl Scouts are able to sell more cookies than ever. The ease of the tools, and the popularity of the cookies make selling to a broad geographically diverse audience possible. As reporter Victor Lukerson writes, the "business strategy is pretty simple: appeal to a large customer base with a quality product."[1] Use that formula, and the cookies practically sell themselves.

Carolyn Blatchey's case study from Cumberland County Library System (Carlisle, Pennsylvania) takes a similarly technological turn. By automating processes and exploiting web tools, the system has made a high-tech response to a budgetary and customer service challenge. By abandoning the idea that good library service means in-person library service, Cumberland County has been able to build a web presence that decreases costs while increasing vital public services.

Moving to Web-Based Services

How Smart Planning and Staff Training Factored into a Complete Website Overhaul—and Improved Community Outreach

Carolyn Blatchley

THE CUMBERLAND COUNTY Library System (CCLS) is a federated system of public libraries in South Central Pennsylvania. Faced with plunging tax revenues, librarians made a radical choice to abandon traditional hands-on services, and refocus staff time and use automated and self-service processes to interact with customers. By reexamining core services to determine which alternative methods or technologies could lead to long-term savings, this case study will describe the ways the CCLS is leveraging web-based services and reallocating the shrinking dollars in its annual budget.

Background

The CCLS consists of seven federated local libraries, one branch facility, a system administrative office located in Carlisle, Pennsylvania, and an associated nonprofit Cumberland County Library System Foundation. On a per capita basis, Cumberland County Library System is the busiest county library system in the Commonwealth of Pennsylvania. More than 2.6 million items were lent to borrowers of all ages in 2010. Annually, more than 1.3 million people visit the library system. With approximately 3,500 people visiting CCLS libraries every day, the CCLS boasts more annual visitors than the combined totals of people who annually visit Carlisle's ten car shows, the state parks in Cumberland County, and U.S. Army Heritage and Educational Center. Over 120,000 people attended free CCLS library programs in 2010.

In the 2006 Taxpayer Return-on-Investment in Pennsylvania Public Libraries Study, Pennsylvania's public libraries boasted a return of $5.50 in benefits for every $1.00 of tax support, or $55 for every $10 in local, state, and federal tax investments to support public libraries.[2]

Despite this statistic, state funding to public libraries has been suffering from cuts to Pennsylvania's public library subsidy, POWER Library reference databases, Ask Here PA (online reference service), the statewide library card program, and interlibrary delivery. Public libraries are not a mandated service in Pennsylvania, and the best way to secure more local support is through the strong incentives in the state aid program.

In 2009–2010, CCLS lost 33 percent of its direct financial state support for library services. This was approximately $721,884 in direct operating support funding, and a cumulative loss of $859,965 in direct operating support. For the 2011 budget year, the state public library subsidy dipped to the nearly the same funding levels as 1999–2000.

As CCLS and its member libraries began to feel the pinch of swift and drastic cuts to revenue, drastic measures had to be taken, including a reduction in operating hours and materials purchasing. Reduced operating hours on the least busy days did not result in layoffs; however, several full-time staff were moved to part-time status, and many part-time employees had their hours reduced. A 10 percent reduction in staff at the member libraries and library system, and a 7 percent increase in volunteers, meant member libraries could keep the doors open and maintain the status quo in terms of services to customers, but more cuts were on the horizon and library services could not be sustained at this rate. Something needed to change at the system level, and we hoped that using the web would provide part of the solution.

History of the CCLS Web Presence

The CCLS administrative office is a department of county government, and is governed by the CCLS system board, while the individual libraries are governed independently. To participate in the library system, each local library board has a membership agreement with the library system board, and local library staff members are employees of the local library.

The library system administrative office provides member libraries with services in six core areas:

1. Administrative and financial services
2. Information technology
3. Technical services (acquisitions, cataloging, processing of library materials)
4. Training services for staff and board members
5. Direct library services
6. Outreach services to older adults

Providing these core services consistently across the county is an important cost-savings goal of the administrative office, and the website is an essential element in leveling the playing field for Cumberland County residents.

One of the most challenging things about creating and maintaining a website for the CCLS is the fact that it is a federated library system. The autonomy of local libraries sometimes competes with the goal to provide a unified presence on the website. To further complicate the situation, until 2008, all website services were provided under the Cumberland County Information Management and Technology Office—a department of county government. The CCLS was required to utilize the same platform as all other county departments, and follow the website style guidelines set for government services.

In 2001, all Cumberland County libraries used Microsoft FrontPage to update websites, with a tedious process that required individual libraries to create content. Content was e-mailed to a single staff member in the library system's Computer Services department. All material had to be approved, often modified, and then uploaded to a centralized server using file transfer protocol (FTP).

Using FrontPage, website changes took days to process, and there was little flexibility in the amount of information libraries could add to the site. In fact, page content was mainly links that were repeated on all member library pages. Libraries had no access to professional, royalty-free stock photos and often relied on clip art images that were ambiguous, and not optimized for the website.

When Cumberland County moved to a content management system in the first quarter of 2004, it adopted Cimbrian's Pennsylvania Dynamic Site Framework (PA DSF), which was being used all over the commonwealth for state and local government websites. The library system still had to work within the confines of county guidelines for websites; however, the new platform provided a much more professional look and feel, and the library editors could update pages in real time with a WYSIWYG editor and customize as permitted by the county.

For the first time, local library staff could upload documents and images rather than send them to a single staff member with upload permissions. More importantly, website work could be divided among staff at the local library, and multiple staff members at the administrative office had access to assist with website services. Dividing the work was very important to CCLS and member libraries, because the 2003–04 budget passed by the state legislature and signed by Governor Rendell called for public libraries to lose 50 percent of their basic operating support for services in 2004 (a supplemental appropriations bill restored some of that funding, but the cut was still approximately 37 percent).

Editing the website became easier with PA DSF, but with navigation dictated by county website rules, the member libraries found that the only way to keep visitors from accidentally leaving the library pages of the website was to duplicate all navigational links on all library landing pages.

Member libraries were maintaining a section of the county website that had:

- no clear audiences,
- irrelevant information for intended communities,
- confusing and complex navigational structures,
- severe duplication, making the user experience unreliable,
- ineffective promotion of top tasks and stories, and
- poorly slanted focus toward the organization rather than the customer.

In fact, an expert review of content on the library web pages found that 68 percent of the content was duplicate material, which created a confusing user experience.

During the summer of 2008, Cumberland County embarked upon another major website redesign, and the CivicPlus Government Content Management System (GCMS) was chosen as the platform. Cumberland County got a well-deserved pat on the back for this redesign. It was selected by the Center for Digital Government (CDG) and the National Association of Counties (NACo) as one of the top ten governmental websites in the nation for counties with populations between 150,000 and 249,000.

The new site provided public access to over 1,600 pages of information, including public records, geographical information, county contracts and meeting minutes, and property ownership and tax records. All county services were described along with contact information. Additions to the county's fourth revision of the website include Archives (Historical Data), solicitation and bid notifications, and online job application capability.

While the platform provided more stability and flexibility than ever, the library system and member libraries continued to find themselves stifled by the content rules of the county government. For example, the site header images, top and left navigation, search features, calendar of events, and home page link were all elements provided by and leading back to the Cumberland County government.

This design definitely did not meet the unique needs of the libraries. Additionally, no library system administrative office staff, or member library staff, were in a position to make changes to page layouts or even authorize editors and Intranet logins to the content management system.

Meanwhile, the web was evolving, including free access to a proliferation of social networking tools. Creative library staff were rumbling about abandoning a united CCLS web presence and instead, creating unique web pages and blogs that would not be part of a unified domain and would not fall under library system branding.

Luckily, long-term strategic planning was on the library system's side. The CCLS administrative office and system board had been in negotiation with Cumberland County to provide a portal to library services, rather than continuing to maintain web pages on the government site. For an interim period, CCLS libraries maintained PA DSF web pages, while the library system administrative office and all county departments moved to CivicPlus.

A Library Services and Technology Act (LSTA) grant was awarded to CCLS, and in mid-2008, the County authorized the library system to begin creating an independent presence on the web. CCLS was able to engage the assistance of a website usability expert and purchase a separate installation of the county's website content management system, taking the first steps on a journey to improve website services.

To the present day, the CCLS administrative office maintains a presence on the Cumberland County website (www.ccpa.net), but only as it relates to government and departmental services. Services to the public and information about individual libraries can now be found on the Cumberland County Library System website (www.cumberlandcountylibraries.org)—a site that undergoes continuous improvement, including another intense website redesign in 2013.

The 2013 iteration of the library system's website is much less expensive to operate, putting thousands of dollars back into an already tight budget. Three administrative office staff members have undertaken the training necessary to administrate a website using Drupal, a free, open-source CMS. CCLS will save additional dollars on website software and related services that had to be purchased outside of the CivicPlus CMS. Best of all, workloads on local library staff will not increase.

How We Work the Web

Two CCLS administrative office core services (information technology and training services) are integral to the creation and maintenance of a system-wide website presence. The information technology staff purchase domain names and website server space, including the maintenance of a content management system and related online services. The training services staff provide ongoing usability testing and content oversight, training documentation, and communication with website editors at member libraries.

While this may sound like a lot of staff effort, in reality it is only a small portion of the job for two full-time and one part-time staff members at the administrative office. Additionally, approximately twenty-five editors are authorized throughout the member libraries. Smaller libraries only have one or two people trained to work on the site, and larger libraries have five or more staff with editing rights. Editors range from library directors and reference librarians to marketing staff and human resources, none of which are centralized in this federated library system.

The CCLS does not require an approval process for new and edited content, but rather relies on all staff editors to follow training and style guidelines. Libraries may have as many trained editors as desired, and even the system administrative office has more than 50 percent of the staff trained to do one or more tasks on the website. Spreading the work across many people has allowed website work to be done more speedily because editors are plentiful. Training is personalized to meet the needs of new editors, ensuring time is well spent learning specific tasks. Training documents are available on the CCLS Intranet and currently through the vendor site. CCLS will provide video tutorials and written documentation for the new Drupal site.

Regular meetings of the CCLS System-wide Website Advisory Team (SWAT) provide a forum for ongoing website evaluation. SWAT is made up of four members from the administrative office staff and one or more members from local libraries. SWAT meets quarterly to:

- recommend changes to website standards and guidelines;
- recommend minimum website maintenance tasks and responsibilities;
- evaluate the current state of the CCLS website; and
- identify areas for improvement and identify new technologies
  and needed functionality for possible adoption.

This team ensures that the website is constantly undergoing statistical and content evaluation, and the style guidelines are open to change based on the current state of website technology.

The CCLS website contains a wealth of "brochure information," and also virtual services to the community. Among these are:

- access the library catalog to browse, place requests, renew items, and pay fines;
- register for a new library card;
- make a purchase suggestion or request a title through Interlibrary Loan;
- log in as an authenticated user to online databases and e-books purchased by Cumberland County, the Capital Area Library District and Common- wealth Libraries;
- obtain readers' advisory services, such as subject-specific newsletters, RSS feeds to updated reading lists, and read-alikes in the catalog;
- sign up for notifications of everything from due date reminders and library news to library jobs and calls for advocacy;
- search and register for library programs and events using a system-wide calendar;
- ask reference questions using an e-mail form to a local staff member, or Ask Here PA (a 24-hour reference service provided by Commonwealth Libraries);
- report lost or stolen library cards and items;
- donate online to any library or the Library System Foundation; and
- interact with the library through social media.

Allowing library customers to perform these tasks online frees up library staff time to focus on direct customer services that can't be performed by machines. Streamlined ILL software was created using open-source software and allows nearly three times as many staff to place requests on behalf of library customers. This ILL software also provides direct communication with the public, which can cancel their own ILL requests and get notifica- tion of pick-up without staff assistance. Online program registration reduced the number of phone calls and paper registrations floating around libraries. Online payments for everything from fines to donations created new avenues for revenue.

Creating a New Website

As a first step to creating a new website, the CCLS administrative office staff and member library staff all agreed to maintain a website that would both simplify and unify virtual access to the collection in service to the community, and foster trust and loyalty through an online experience that is relevant, reliable, and error-free. This was both a customer service commitment and a cost-savings measure.

The CCLS staff educated themselves by attending website related sessions at conferences sponsored by the Pennsylvania Library Association and the Public Library Association, and at Computers in Libraries. Through professional literature and training experiences, the staff began to make notes about best practices in website design, and specifically, websites designed to meet the needs of public library constituents.

Through the procurement of 2008 LSTA funds and matching library dollars, CCLS obtained proposals for usability testing and staff education. The CCLS ultimately chose to work with Kathy McShae of Emerald Strategies, Inc. The proposal included actions, such as:

- auditing the old site,
- assessing user needs,
- usability testing of the site before and after migration,
- suggesting tools for improved design and testing of the site,
- creating wireframes for the content management system,
- acting as an advocate to ensure the content management system fulfilled the library system needs, and
- training staff to continuously assess the usability of the CCLS site.

The proposal promised CCLS would get actionable results to measure progress, align with industry best practices, and lead with facts, rather than opinions, focusing research-based website orientation.

Emerald Strategies saved an enormous amount of staff time and effort by providing best practices examples for content elements and language, and training the website editing staff in these areas. Additionally, library staff were instilled with the value of continuously examining the site for consistency, readability, and usability errors, and they were given free or low-cost tools to ensure these goals were met. Leading into a 2013 complete website redesign project, the System-wide Website Advisory Team keeps usability at the forefront of their planning.

FIG. 2.1

Best Practices	Voice of Customer	Voice of Stakeholder
Expert review scorecard	User interview	Planning assessment
Requirements	Customer profile	Design strategy
Benchmark	Task analysis baseline	Information architecture
		Training and publication guide

The scope of usability was outlined in ten elements on three distinct areas (see figure 2.1):

1. identifying Best Practices,
2. hearing the Voice of the Customer, and
3. hearing the Voice of the Stakeholders.

Emerald Strategies set up a design strategy for CCLS with benchmarks for identifying:

- business goals,
- branding goals,
- target users,
- general website tasks,
- critical success factors, and
- technology constraints.

Plans for reviewing the site, finding out what the residents of Cumberland County needed from the library website, and what the staff and new content management system were able to do through planning, design, and training were key to the process. A design strategy based on branding provided focus on reversing the weaknesses identified by the expert site review and user interviews, and allowed the website team to lead with the strengths users attribute to the CCLS.

Design Strategy 1: Business Goals

CCLS member libraries and key library system administrative office staff participated in exercises that identified the business goals of the website. Emerald

Strategies outlined the value those goals bring to the website, and the visual strategies CCLS would need to implement to meet those goals.

Design Strategy 2: Branding Goal

The branding goal was an opportunity for the CCLS to tie the website together with a single, memorable phrase. This phrase was placed within the wireframe at the top left-hand corner of the website, and was intended to bring identity to the unified presence the administrative office, the member libraries, and the myriad virtual services brought to CCLS.

While other libraries and organizations were adopting the trendy "three word tagline" where each word is separated by periods, CCLS decided the overly simplistic message would lessen the potential impact.

The final tagline became exactly what this site was setting out to be: Library Services All in One Place.

Design Strategy 3: Target Users

Emerald Strategies worked with the CCLS staff to identify just four groups of target users, but this was nearly impossible, given the scope of a public library system's core constituency. To date, the CCLS website continues to focus on six key groups of users:

1. kids
2. teens
3. parents
4. adults
5. older adults
6. homebound individuals

Design Strategy 4: General Website Tasks

This is the design strategy that really got CCLS website editors thinking about usability. By conducting surveys, studying library customer behaviors, and performing usability tests on the website, library staff were able to create customer profiles and identify a hierarchy to the navigational structure of the new website.

Library staff identified why people used the library, including the website, and the top tasks they were performing. This was not a measure of their success, rather a close examination of what the public wanted from the library (see figure 2.2).

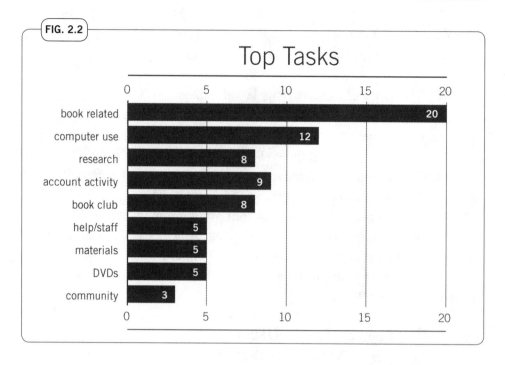

FIG. 2.2

Top Tasks

Using this data, Emerald Strategies created seven scenarios to see how effectively and efficiently the library system website met the users' needs, by having them perform top tasks and rate user satisfaction and productivity. Through guided scenarios, users were asked specific questions that showed whether or not they could:

- determine library locations and hours,
- find out about library programs and register online,
- find the answer to a question, such as how fines are assessed,
- receive reading recommendations,
- place requests on items,
- renew items already checked out, and
- find out about library activities and new purchases via newsletters.

Emerald Strategies used identical testing questions and methods to collect baseline data on the PA DSF site, and to beta test the new site the library system built on the CivicPlus platform independent of the county government website (see figure 2.3).

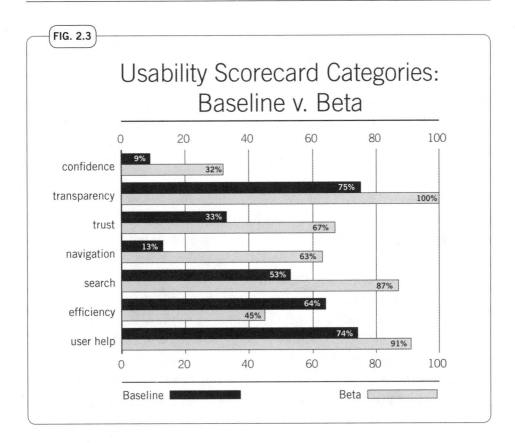

FIG. 2.3

Usability Scorecard Categories: Baseline v. Beta

Category	Baseline	Beta
confidence	9%	32%
transparency	75%	100%
trust	33%	67%
navigation	13%	63%
search	53%	87%
efficiency	64%	45%
user help	74%	91%

Baseline ▬▬▬ Beta ▭▭▭

Design Strategy 5: Critical Success Factors

Next, Emerald Strategies led CCLS staff through a series of exercises that helped library staff identify what success looked like—not just for the website debut in 2008, but to carry CCLS into the future.

Creating success measurements ensured all content editors and people of influence over the website were held to the same set of standards. These involved:

Becoming a standards-based organization

- Just as libraries adhere to strict standards of cataloging, and past CCLS web pages adhered to the standards of the county government website, the new library system website needed to have specific taxonomies, a website publishing guide, and staff access to resources to meet these standards (such as a subscription service to high-quality images, and the ability to edit the images).
- These standards were created with best practices for library websites in mind, and all libraries agreed to them before adoption. The CCLS System-wide Website Advisory Team periodically examines and adapts

these standards, and CCLS administrative office staff use them for train-ing and ongoing maintenance of the site.

Making the website essential to organizational culture

- The library system examined the roles of library users and successfully aligned online and offline content. It has taken some time, but many of the tasks that a person can perform in the library can now be done using virtual services.
- While the website will not replace the human level of service or the sense of place found in a physical library, members of the public can perform more tasks online and after hours than ever before.

Using the website to promote library activities

- Until the creation of this website, it was often difficult and time consum-ing to post information to the web. Living up to the tagline "Library Ser-vices All in One Place," website editors, programming staff, and market-ing staff all began to utilize the website as a storage space for detailed information on anything being promoted via newsletter, flyer, Facebook, or other means. The website also became a space for promoting library newsletters, and a social media presence.

Design Strategy 6: Technology Constraints

While CCLS was granted the ability to break away from the county website, the content management system (CMS) remained the same platform, which is very well designed to meet the needs of government entities, such as counties and local municipalities, but it is not as friendly to public libraries.

The CCLS staff had no single staff member named as "Web Master" and no single staff member with the technology skills to put library vendors through the paces to integrate all library services. Emerald Strategies acted as an advo-cate, giving CCLS the words and a voice in making this site work.

Challenges included:

1. Integration of the public access catalog, Horizon Information Portal (HIP) from SirsiDynix—the final solution requires users to link to a cus-tomized version of HIP with a similar appearance as the CCLS website, which opens in a new window.

2. Database integration, in that CCLS could not avoid a jarring experience for those needing to be authenticated as users, and no means of fully branding the library databases. These links also open in a new window.

3. Underperformance from certain browsers. The CMS was initially designed with Internet Explorer as the intended browser, and website usability testing was performed using Firefox add-ons, and therefore the Firefox browser.

4. Full compliance with ADA website accessibility requirements for the website. This goal was unachievable due to the nature of hardcoded elements within the CMS, and CCLS staff continue to implement best practices where able.

Emerald Strategies left CCLS with five important low-tech documents:

1. Website Scorecard to grade the site against usability best practices,
2. Design Strategy to keep everyone on the same page,
3. Planning Assessment Grid to use as a strategic roadmap,
4. Web Governance System to framework the strategy, and
5. Publication Guidelines to use as a desktop reference for content standards.

Three high-tech tools were used in the planning process:

1. Basecamp provided an online project management site.
2. Usability Testing Environment (UTE) provided an easy way to do streamlined task analysis.
3. GoToMeeting enabled remote online meetings and recording of remote usability testing.

Conclusion

Moving to the web worked; online services, self-services, partnerships, energy efficiencies, and creative funding sources all contributed to most Cumberland County member libraries reinstating hours in 2012. Additionally, CCLS libraries began implementing efficient services that rely less on staff time. CCLS libraries have moved away from staffing structures that centralize certain jobs and services to structures that eliminate bottlenecks with shared workloads. While moving more to web-based services hasn't solved all of the CCLS' challenges, the move to abandon traditional structures and ideas about library services has enabled us to better serve our community.

Bookend

The French chef Fernand Point is famous for saying, "Success is the sum of a lot of small things done correctly," and by this measure, Cumberland County Library System has made a success out of a budgetary nightmare. By treating their web presence as a "virtual branch," automating processes, and focusing on training, the system created a new philosophy and service mindset. This mindset saves the library—and the patrons—time and money, freeing up resources to focus on core services requiring more in-person contact. Despite catastrophic budget cuts, the library continues to focus on accountability and service to their core constituencies.

We're not advocating for putting the entire library experience online—not everything can or should be digitized. But focusing on smart planning and staff training is giving the Cumberland County enhanced flexibility and improved outreach.

Chef Point also famously said, "Butter! Give me butter! Always butter!" These are not days of butter for public libraries, and sometimes it seems that even margarine must be scarce. But the Cumberland County Library System's case study shows one way to allocate shrinking budget dollars while continuing to make a positive impact on the libraries' community.

REFERENCES

1. Victor Luckerson, "Girl Scouts Use Social Media, Mobile Tech to Break Cookie Sales Records," *Time.com*, November 2, 2012, accessed November 12, 2012, http://business.time.com/2012/11/02/girl-scouts-use-social-media-mobile-tech-to-break-cookie-sales-records.

2. Jose-Marie Griffiths, et al. "Taxpayer Return on Investment (ROI) in Pennsylvania Public Libraries" UNC School of Information and Library Sciences, September 2006, accessed November 28, 2012, www.ila.org/advocacy/pdf/UNC_Pennsylvania.pdf.

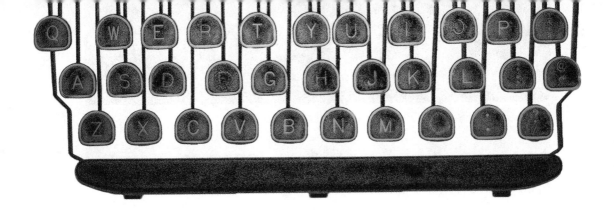

| Case Study 3 | # University of Arizona Libraries |

IMAGINE AN ACADEMIC library. Now imagine an academic library without a reserves service desk. In fact, without reserve service at all. If you keep imagining, you may come up with something like the current reality at the University of Arizona.

The University of Arizona's innovations in service and team-based organizational strategies have been making library news since 1994. The following case study by Robyn Huff-Eibl and Jeanne Voyles highlights one radical piece of abandonment: eliminating all physical and print reserve services in an academic research library. Huff-Eibl and Voyles offer a comprehensive, fourteen-year overview of how much time and dedication to continuous change and analysis it takes to abandon what had been a signature library service. Keep in mind that librarians at the University of Arizona didn't approach the issue knowing that they would ultimately eliminate all reserves. The service went through several iterations and changes along the way. The key to their decision was committing to a process improvement cycle that allows all services to be regularly assessed, evaluated, and perhaps abandoned.

In a recent exchange on Wayne Bivens-Tatum's Academic Librarian blog, Barbara Fister, Librarian at Gustavus Adolphus College, argues, "I think librarians haven't innovated in big ways because we think local and have underestimated our own value." We could also add that the refusal to abandon past practices has held us back; we cannot innovate while continuing all of our past practices.[1]

The University of Arizona is clearly asking Drucker's question: "If we did not do this already, would we go into it now?" And here is their answer.

Being Relevant in the 21st Century

Elimination of Physical and Electronic Reserve Services

Robyn Huff-Eibl and Jeanne F. Voyles

We would like to acknowledge and thank members of the Access and Information Services and Delivery, Description and Acquisition Teams, along with the numerous project teams focused on customer service, process improvement, and willingness to embrace change and fear.

Introduction

In this case study, the University of Arizona Libraries (UAL) will present the approach and process we took to evaluate and abandon our print and electronic reserve services. We will discuss outcomes, challenges faced, and lessons learned in our evolution from these traditional legacy services to our core service concept of "Everywhere you are: the Library."

Background

UAL is a public research institution with four separate locations across a campus of 38,000 students. Over the past 15 years, similar to other academic libraries, the UAL budget has experienced significant cuts, including the loss of over 30 classified staff and librarian positions and no state-funded increase in the acquisitions budget.[2]

At the same time that cuts were occurring, UAL also experienced increased pressure to demonstrate value to library users by meeting and, in order to survive, exceeding their needs. Fortunately, in 1993, UAL went through a significant reorganization which resulted in the adoption of values such as customer focus and continual improvement. Following the 1993 reorganization, a major effort to train library staff on Total Quality Management (TQM) and Process Improvement (PI) methodology was implemented and applied to areas of service in which we were receiving increased complaints.[3] One of those services was reserves, both books and photocopied articles. The goal of this initial project was to improve turnaround time of processed reserve items while reducing costs. We did not envision at that time that in future years we would eliminate this service all together. Instead we kept focused on the voice of the customer and the improvement of services which led to the creation of seven project teams, over the course of 14 years, focused on improved customer service and continuous improvement that positioned us to make the decision in 2008 to "plan for the abandonment" of reserves, both physical and electronic. The eight project teams were:

- 1995: Reserve Process Improvement (focused on service quality and efficiency)
- 1998–2009: UAL implemented five different versions of electronic reserves
- 1998: Electronic Reserve Process Improvement Project Team (from paper copies of articles to an electronic reserve process)
- 2000: Transitioned instructors from POLIS to OSCR (database managed by UAL)
- 2002: Electronic Delivery Analysis Team (EDAT) which transitioned instructors from OSCR to ERes software
- 2006: Stream Team (implementation of streaming media)
- 2008: Migrating all Electronic Reserves (ERes) requests to campus course management system (CMS)
- 2008: Physical Reserves Abandonment Project

What we learned over the course of fourteen years and eight project teams later was being relevant in the 21st century not only means meeting customer needs but also examining our traditional services and service models for continued 21st century relevance.

History of Reserve Process Improvement

Our journey to improve reserve processes began in 1995 when a PI project team, composed of both classified staff and librarians knowledgeable about the process and members not involved in the process who could offer a neutral outside perspective, was formed. This principle is still applied to the formation of PI and other project teams at UAL today. Regardless of the library's well-laid plan to communicate to faculty the need to submit reserve requests by a designated date, the majority of requests came in days before the semester began creating huge backlogs of material to process. The most significant outcome of this extensive study to review the reserve process was implementing a plan to "staff to the work," making changes in staffing patterns to accommodate the peak of each semester and implement a quality standard addressing turnaround time which would guarantee faculty when their assigned readings would be processed and available to students. The quality standard implemented guaranteed that within 24 to 48 hours of receipt of material assigned readings would be processed and ready for checkout by their students. Scheduling to our peak became an operating norm across the library for this as well as other services. Work schedules were changed to meet the demands of the work rather than when library staff wanted to work. Because of the huge volume of reserves to be processed in a relatively short period of time, temporary staff was added, and cross-training of additional classified staff as well as student assistants was implemented to accomplish this work. This staffing model and changes in process contributed greatly to the library consistently meeting quality standards which were reported out to the library on a regular basis.

Why is it important to focus on this initial PI project when thinking about abandoning a service? For UAL, this laid the foundation for our future thinking and planning when addressing service issues, improving a process, and investigating other alternatives for providing a service. In addition to applying TQM principles, UAL has also worked over the years to create a culture of assessment as a way to efficiently and effectively keep up with changing user expectations.[4] In a culture of assessment, needs assessment and evaluation are not seen as one-time efforts nor can one assume they know what is best for the customers without asking or observing. Data collection and analysis that included customer feedback became central to the decision-making processes at UAL. Needs assessment and PI methodologies are a thread that is woven throughout our organization and allow us to evaluate our services and provide an opportunity to study and create new services to implement based on the changing needs and demands of our customers.

Our second in a series of five PI projects pertaining to electronic reserves was charged to study and implement electronic reserves. Moving from paper reserves to assigned articles available electronically in PDF required a major shift for faculty. Once a decision was made by the team to move forward with the first electronic reserves service utilizing an on-campus system called POLIS, the team created an implementation plan which included an extensive communication plan to faculty and students regarding the elimination of paper reserves.

The communication plan developed by the project team focused on the benefits of electronic reserves, one obvious benefit for our students was electronic readings being available 24/7. Essential learnings from this project that contributed to the success were providing faculty enough time to transition to electronic reserves and extensive training on the new system and subsequent systems. Library staff were consistently available for faculty to support a successful transition and did whatever was required to make it happen. There were instances where there were technical difficulties both within the library and on campus. We made a commitment early on that we would not bounce customers all over campus and within the library. Regardless of the issue, library staff (day, night, or weekend) would take the lead to make the appropriate contacts and find solutions to faculty issues and communicate back to faculty in a timely fashion.

Between 1998 and 2009, the library implemented five different versions of electronic reserves, each one providing improvements and new enhancements driven by technology that met the information needs of our students. With each version, our library staff worked with library systems staff and outside vendors to make changes requested by customers, trained library classified staff and librarians on new processes, and educated faculty and students by phone, e-mail, and in person on a daily basis. The foundation and process utilized to transition to electronic reserves was later used in 2008 when the library made the decision to plan for the abandonment and elimination of electronic reserves, providing instead canned articles that faculty could link to their individual websites and or course page in the campus CMS.

Before we arrived at the 2008 decision to abandon the reserve processes, another vital restructuring change in 2002 led to the merging of delivery of electronic services and all similar services into one team with a focus on distance learning students. In 2001-2002, the Customer-Oriented Library Realignment (COLA) project team was formed to strategically look at the structure of the library in anticipation of new work and services that could be implemented within a five-year period. Out of that team's work, a project team was formed to analyze and study the feasibility of implementing document delivery services. As a result of their work and the approval of Library Cabinet (administrators and governance representatives), the Document Delivery Team (DDT) was formed and merged Photocopy (similar to the Kinkos business, however, not supported by state funds), electronic reserves, and interlibrary loan into one team. Previously this work was assigned to two distinct teams in the library. With this new team structure came challenges related to reserve services as the electronic and physical reserve services were now assigned to two different teams, leaving physical reserves part of the Materials Access Team (now known as the Access and Information Services Team, AIST).

With this separation, and our organization's team-based values to break down silos and work towards the benefit of library users, both teams realized an opportunity to work together to present a seamless service to our customers. In early January 2004, one reserve website was created as a resource for faculty and students. Similar to every other restructuring, with the formation of DDT, the Electronic Delivery Analysis Team (EDAT) was formed in September 2002, and was charged with analyzing existing work processes in DDT, investigating ways to streamline or replace existing processes, and developing new and improved processes and resources for electronic delivery of materials. Data analyzed from 1998–2007 showed that the electronic reserve service grew from supporting a few hundred classes in 1998 to over 1,200 in fiscal year 2006–2007. We believe the increase over these years was due to the convenience to our faculty in submitting requests electronically and faculty understanding the value and efficiency for students in having electronic access to assigned readings 24/7. The service became more popular when we implemented our document delivery services and pulled items from our collection to be scanned for course assignments. During this time, no new staff was reallocated to meet the increased demands for this service. We implemented the following strategies to address the increased workloads: staff cross-trained across DDT to support all services, work schedules adjusted, and temporary staff hired for ER peak period. The outcomes of EDAT were systems analysis resulting in the purchase and implementation of ERes software, a pilot program of color scanning and streaming audio for the Fine Arts department in fall 2003 and campus-wide in spring 2004. Ultimately, the savings from merging services and PI initiatives resulted in a savings of $8,400 in student wages and one full-time classified staff position that were returned to the library for reallocation or budget cuts.

Physical Reserves

While several PI projects were occurring for electronic reserves, physical reserves were also undergoing data collection and process improvement. In 2003, with the focus on unmediated access and ultimately better service for library users, UAL began examining space allocation and usage of physical reserves. We quickly began to discover many physical items placed on reserve were never touched from semester to semester. In order to communicate resource constraints with faculty, we created a policy that prohibited items left on physical reserves permanently, and we began implementing a limit of 75 physical items, per course, allowed on reserve each semester. This reduced some of the resources allocated for processing items that were never used.

The review of physical reserve statistics, coupled with students who would approach the reserve desk and ask for the "blue book on the bottom shelf," staff knowledge of PI, the implementation of self-checkout machines, shrinking resources, and the merging of public service desks made us question our traditional assumptions regarding "why do we keep physical reserves and books on hold behind a counter forcing customers to wait in line?" In 2004, after surveying various listservs to inquire whether or not anyone had placed their physical reserves or hold books out in the open, there was no academic library that had abandoned this fear, and many were resistant to the thought, including UAL staff. There were however, large public libraries that were placing items on hold out in the public space for users to pick up and check out themselves. In 2004, starting at the Fine Arts Library (the smallest UAL branch), we experimented with open holds and open physical reserves. We placed physical reserve (153 items) and hold books in an area adjacent to the public service desk but out in the open allowing unmediated customer access. After one year of no issues and no faculty or user concerns, we implemented this in 2005 at the Science-Engineering Library (our second largest UAL branch, 259 reserve items). With this implementation, we surveyed science faculty and the only concern was confidentiality and not associating their names with the requested title due to competition of grants. However, they did not care whether or not physical reserve items were out on the public shelves. To solve the confidentiality problem and save overall resources, we decided not to wrap hold books and instead place them in call number order, similar to how the physical reserve books were shelved, on open public shelves next to the reserve books. Other than the multiple copies of faculty-owned math and chemistry textbooks that wandered throughout the library and on occasion were lost or stolen, no other problems occurred at the Science-Engineering Library. The math and chemistry textbooks (roughly 20 to 30 items) were eventually placed behind the Science-Engineering public service desk, but all other reserve books were kept in the open for unmediated customer access. In 2006, overcoming our fears, we decided to implement unmediated access to physical reserves at the Main Library. This collection totaled 1,990 items. Ultimately, the implementation of open book reserves allowed for the consolidation of multiple service points into single public service desks and the migration of classified staff to the single all-purpose public desk at the Science-Engineering Library.

While initially placing all VHS and DVD's (whether on reserve or not) out in the public worked, over time the theft rate increased to a point where replacing the items was more costly than physically processing them for reserves. Rather than abandon our open access strategy, we forced ourselves to again think about the library users. Having open access to the VHS and DVD collection was helpful but it did not allow for simultaneous viewing, which was the time-saver students were seeking. In 2006, we created a project team called Stream Team that was charged with investigating and implementing a streaming media service to support classes taught on campus. Initially, UAL piloted a streaming service partnering with the campus Learning Technology Center (LTC) using existing campus technology. When this did not meet our quality standard expectations, we moved to piloting Cdigix and eventually settled on the implementation of Video Furnace (now called Haivision).

The UAL has always adhered to our collection development policy that we do not purchase textbooks to add to the collection or borrow textbooks for students through our interlibrary loan service. UAL has never been funded to support the purchase of textbooks and in reality could never purchase enough textbooks to serve a campus of 38,000. We do believe working to reduce the costs and increase accessibility of course material (textbooks, books, readings, video or audio, and software) for students is an important issue. For the past several years we have been working in partnership with our undergraduate and graduate library advisory groups and various campus groups (bookstore, Student Affairs, Office of Instructional Assessment, and individual faculty and faculty senate) to explore alternatives to physical textbooks and course readings to reduce the costs and increase efficiencies for our students. In the fall of 2012, UAL charged a project team to facilitate the campus moving to a more holistic and coordinated approach to identifying, acquiring, and delivering required course materials and services.

With the migration toward scanned assigned readings and the implementation of audio and media reserves, usage of the physical reserve collection, as expected, experienced a steep decline. By 2007, most items remaining on physical reserve were either never used or had fewer than five uses, including in-house use. For example, at the Science-Engineering Library 71 percent of all reserve items were checked out or used in-house five times or less (278 items on reserve with 198 items used in-house or checked out less than five times). This data matched reserve circulation and in-house data at the Main and Fine Arts Libraries and increased in 2008. Data collected at the end of Spring Semester 2008 indicated 88 percent of physical materials on reserve in the Main Library, 81 percent at Science-Engineering, and 96 percent at Fine Arts circulated and/or were used in-house less than five times. In an attempt to further communicate with faculty about staff resources required to process physical reserves and the continued lack of use of physical reserve books, AIST began communicating usage statistics to faculty at the end of each semester so they were aware of the usage of the items they placed on physical reserves. This final piece of data and the need for additional classified staff resources on the Main Library Information Commons public reference desk became the critical factors which led the 2007 Library-Wide Restructuring Team and Library Cabinet to make the decision to abandon both our course physical and electronic reserve services on June 30, 2009. Ultimately, this change resulted in the reallocation of 0.5 FTE classified staff to staff the Main Library Information Commons Desk during the evening hours, freeing up librarians to focus on new work such as increased outreach, grant participation, repository, and digitization efforts.

Planned Abandonment

With the significant increase in electronic reserves described earlier, you may be puzzled why we began investigating the possible elimination of our reserve services. In 2002, UAL purchased and began having library employees view the video, "Leading in a Time of Change."[5] This was our first introduction to the concept of "planned abandonment" as an essential idea necessary to assist in leading change. Organizations and leaders tend to hold on to what is known and familiar, but Drucker "calls for planned abandonment, which involves knowing when to stop doing what no longer works. Ask yourself, if we weren't already doing this today, would it make sense to start?"[6] If not, plan abandonment rather than prolong the inevitable. As stated by Stoffle, Leeder and Sykes-Casavant in their article, "Bridging the Gap: Wherever you are, The Library," "The primary purpose of this perspective is to eliminate projects or programs before they go into decline with the purpose of freeing up those resources—staff, financial, and otherwise—to pursue new, more innovative projects that will move the organization forward."

In the middle of our reserves process improvement journey, we were intrigued by University of California, Merced (UCM) Library's conscious decision not to offer a traditional physical reserve service when they opened in 2005, instead focusing on building their digital library. Around this same time, UAL was approached by two student senators from the Associated Students of the University of Arizona (ASUA) who requested the library's assistance in consolidating all assigned course readings in the campus CMS. After all, they figured, that is where the students most needed them. At that time, electronic readings and course materials were available from a variety of places, depending on the course (e.g., faculty websites, CMS, and library website). With the seeds of "planned abandonment" firmly planted, UCM Library's opening without traditional physical reserves, the voice of our customers desiring one access point to locate their assigned readings, and additional budget cuts in 2007–2008, the time was right and we were positioned to make the decision for "planned abandonment."

In the summer of 2008, two final reserve project teams were formed. The Physical Reserves Abandonment Project Team addressed the yearlong transition of faculty no longer utilizing course physical reserves. The second project team was charged with the migration of all ERes requests to the campus CMS. This project was appointed to design a process and assist faculty in managing their own electronic resources through the campus CMS. To begin this project, UAL initially partnered with faculty willing to pilot the transition of linking their assigned readings to their course page within the campus CMS. During this transition, many faculty had not yet begun using the campus CMS. In order to support their successful transition, the project team partnered with LTC and learned how to use the campus CMS in order to provide training for faculty. Taking the approach to work through logistical and technical glitches with a pilot group first was a key strategy to this project's success when scaling up the implementation to the entire campus. This required working with 1,420 faculty representing 1,780 courses and 26,883 files, zipped by DDT staff to assist in the migration.

Overall we want to acknowledge that this was a major transition for faculty, many of whom were comfortable with the status quo. We also do not want to downplay the years of creating a culture focused on customer self-sufficiency and in particular students' desire for improved consolidated services. Our training to learn TQM and PI techniques, creating a culture of assessment and the determination of our classified staff to overcome barriers and persevere implementing difficult changes, such as planned abandonment, led to the evolution of our success.

LEARNINGS

It is important to acknowledge that throughout this journey there were many challenges to overcome, and in lieu of giving up because it was too overwhelming, technology issues were too challenging, or resistance by some faculty and library staff was too hard, we viewed those challenges as opportunities. One strategy was to present faculty and students with realistic facts regarding the declining budget situation and refocus their attention on the positive outcome for the customer that included improving services and reducing costs. We often asked how as an organization we could move forward with our mission, vision, and strategic plans for the future and overcome these barriers we faced along the way.

Some struggles with the abandonment of physical reserves came from faculty in the humanities where their focus was primarily art images. When appropriate, we investigated other options such as placing key titles in our reference area as non-circulating. On other occasions librarians worked with faculty to explore alternatives to selected monographs, purchased electronic versions if available, or suggested scanning the assigned readings to embed within campus CMS. Not in all, but in most cases faculty were able to make this transition. As stated by Stoffle and others, "This is a difficult challenge for librarians, as we typically hesitate to end a service even if there is one person in our entire community who uses it. We must acknowledge that programs and services used by only one person, or a small number of people, are draining away resources that could be used to create new, improved services that would be more successful and benefit larger numbers of people."[7]

Some struggles with the migration of the ERes to the campus CMS are discussed above, but additionally, in 2007, with realized savings from physical reserves process improvement, we were able to absorb the implementation of a new Express Retrieval Service where we pulled the physical items to be placed on the hold shelf or to be scanned and e-mailed for faculty to upload to the campus CMS. This is another example where we offered a solution to help ease faculty's transition to a new process.

We do not want to minimize the fear that some staff expressed regarding the elimination of a service thinking it would result in job layoffs. To combat this fear the Dean developed a Policy and Procedures for Personnel Reassignment and Layoffs document emphasizing, "All efforts will be made to retain employees. This means employees must be willing to change duties, and/or teams and for classified staff their classification. Employees must be committed to learning all new work assigned to them."

Other key learnings include:

- While change can be difficult for some users, it is welcomed for others.
- Form teams made up of both classified staff and librarians throughout the library.
- Utilize data regarding usage.
- Listen to your customers regarding their desired service.
- Follow TQM principles and PI methodology.
- Think outside the box—break down barriers.
- Challenge traditional methods of providing services by asking the ques-

tions, "If we weren't already doing this today, would it make sense to start?" and "How would you design the service in the 21st Century?"
- Focus on improving areas heavily utilized by customers and areas that tie to library strategic plans.
- Creature a culture of customer focus, continuous improvement, and needs assessment.
- Support staff, by freeing up time so that they can focus on priority projects.
- Utilize project management training to create strong project managers and sponsors that can lead and keep the team focused by continually articulating the purpose, vision, and scope of the project, remove barriers, meet tight deadlines, seek feedback, and communicate progress both library- and campus-wide as needed.
- Celebrate successes along the way.

Conclusion

Like other academic libraries in the late 20th century, UAL offered physical (e.g., books, audio, and video) and electronic course reserve services. This service has long been a faculty tradition and deeply rooted with faculty culture. Over the course of 14 years, we systematically studied and continually improved the usage and customer needs of our physical and electronic reserve services. Through these processes, we moved from having audio materials on physical reserve to digital audio streaming, from physical booking of videos for course use to asynchronous, online video streaming 24/7. The UAL values of customer focus and continual improvement, along with continual budget cuts, forced us to examine all of our work processes while still offering our customers new services. While "planned abandonment" is intended to be applied systematically when examining all processes, every product and service, every procedure and every policy, UAL has only been truly successful in this one case. We have reduced some reliance of other traditional services such as in-house cataloging with the assistance of outsourcing and face-to-face instruction by embedding a one-credit course within some English classes; however, in the case of instruction, pressure remains for traditional ways.[8] With shrinking resources, all organizations must be willing and able to reallocate existing resources from legacy services to the new or changing work. In planning for future needs, we must challenge our perceptions, be strategic, and evaluate services by focusing on costs vs. usage, return on investment, and the overall service value to the customer. Ultimately, we were able to abandon all physical reserves and also migrate all electronic reserves from a stand-alone, in-house system to the campus CMS.

As of 2011, UAL is the only academic library nationally that has and actually eliminated both print and electronic course reserve services.[9] Three years after this decision, the changes and alternatives provided remain relevant today.

Bookend

HUFF-EIBL AND VOYLES indicate that although their library has been explicitly using Peter Drucker's planned abandonment principles for over a decade, the reserve process is the only service actually eliminated. Other services have, however, been modified, outsourced or altered in meaningful ways.

It's time for libraries of all types to start asking themselves hard questions about the relevance and value of services of all types. The process takes perseverance, and often the answer will be "Of course! Yes! We need to continue this service." Asking the question ensures that we keep a critical eye on what matters the most to our organizations, our patrons, and our boards. It was encouraging to see that at a recent presentation on Planned Abandonment in Libraries, participants (mostly public librarians) had no problem determining services to place under scrutiny. The following word cloud outlines the key services identified by participants as possible candidates for a planned abandonment evaluation:

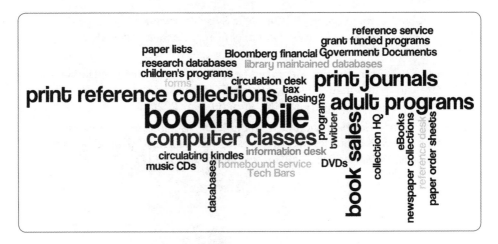

While the thought of abandoning some of these services seems shocking at the outset, remember that we asked for programs that needed to be evaluated carefully, and it would be hard to argue to not evaluate services such as a bookmobile or computer classes or adult programs. A true Drucker disciple would evaluate all services and programs on a periodic basis; in reality you might want to pick and choose, but don't forget that sometimes our most successful services are the ones most in need of attention. The University of Arizona Libraries approached their service analysis without fear, without reservations, and with success.

REFERENCES

1. Wayne Bivens-Tatum, February 13, 2012, "Libraries and the Commodification of Culture," Academic Librarian Blog, http://blogs.princeton.edu/librarian/2012/02/libraries-and-the-commodification-of-culture.

2. Carla J. Stoffle and Cheryl Cuillier,"From Striving to Thriving," *Journal of Library Administration* 51, no. 1 (2011): 130–155.

3. Linda Dols et al., "A Process Improvement Approach to Interlibrary Loan," in Books to Bytes: Contributed Papers Presented at the AzLA 1995 Annual Conference, Phoenix, AZ, November 1995, 10–27.

4. Amos Lakos and Shelley E. Phipps, "Creating a Culture of Assessment: A Catalyst for Organizational Change," *Portal: Libraries and the Academy* 4, no. 3 (2004): 345–361.

5. Peter F. Drucker, Peter M. Senge, Frances Hesselbein, and Peter F. Drucker Foundation for Nonprofit Management. *Leading in a Time of Change: A Conversation with Peter F. Drucker and Peter M. Senge* (San Francisco: Jossey-Bass, 2001).

6. Karl Albrecht, *The Power of Minds at Work: Organizational Intelligence in Action* (New York: AMACON, 2003), 129.

7. Carla J. Stoffle, Kim Leeder, and Gabrielle Sykes-Casavant, "Bridging the Gap: Wherever you are, the Library," *Journal of Library Administration* 48, no. 1 (2008): 19.

8. Rebecca Blackiston, Yvonne Mery, and Leslie Sult, "Developing an Online Credit-Bearing Information Fluency Course: Lessons Learned." Presented at LOEX Conference, Albuquerque, NM, April 30–May 2, 2009.

9. Kymberly Anne Goodson and Linda Frederiksen, "E-Reserves in Transition: Exploring New Possibilities in E-Reserves Service Delivery," *Journal of Interlibrary Loan, Document Delivery Electronic Reserve* 21, no. 1-2 (2011): 33–56.

Case Study 4 | # Oregon State University

PROVIDING MEDIATION HAS always been a librarian's mission—after all, what is a reference interview if not a mediation service? We are asked a question, and we go back and forth with the patron, mediating possible sources, solutions, and angles to approach a solution. But what happens when we need to mediate ourselves—to find a path through our own cognitive biases and move beyond "magical thinking" to critically examine some of our core legacy services?

As librarians, we need to have the intellectual honesty to recognize that we are biased when we start to evaluate our own services. That doesn't, of course, mean we can't address those biases and move forward by pulling apart and examining how our own (natural, normal) biases impact the way we address change.

In Cheryl Middleton's case study of Oregon State University's reference services, we see how one academic librarian worked with colleagues to approach the changing reference needs of her institution from an economic and philosophical standpoint.

Magical Thinking
Moving Beyond Natural Bias to Examine Core Services

Cheryl Middleton

ACADEMIC LIBRARIES HAVE been struggling to keep up with the changing needs of the faculty and students at our institutions for as many years as there have been academic institutions and libraries. As our users' needs change, we must consider whether practices that used to be efficient and effective have become too expensive—taking up resources that we could be using to try new things.

In public services, some of the most contentious discussions of this sort have focused on traditional reference services. What is the economic and philosophical value of continuing to staff reference desks with library faculty, valuable resources who are "waiting" for reference questions to come to them?

Background on OSU Libraries

By 2008, Oregon State University (OSU) Libraries was at a crossroads regarding the most effective use of our library faculty and library spaces to meet the needs of a changing information landscape. OSU Libraries was grappling with an increased demand and acquisition of digital collections, shifting our emphasis from owning collections to accessing collections and engaging in educating the OSU community regarding scholarly communication, open access, and author's rights. Our expanded and remodeled library building that opened in 1999 was already beginning to feel the strain of an increased student population and the need for additional collaborative and quiet study environments for our students. To address these demands and challenges and to align ourselves with OSU strategic goals, we engaged in a library reorganization; reference librarians were split into two departments: Undergraduate Learning and Library Information Access (ULLIA) and Research and Instruction (RIS). The administration and management of the reference desk resided in the ULLIA department. The staffing pool for reference coverage consisted of twelve faculty librarians, three paraprofessionals, eight to ten student assistants, and seven part-time librarians who filled in as needed for vacation and regularly scheduled library faculty meetings. Faculty librarians from RIS and ULLIA were responsible for developing and implementing new reference services, providing reference service to users, and overseeing the reference collection. Together, these departments worked to integrate our print reference collection into the circulating stacks.

At the same time, OSU Libraries administration was calling for change. RIS and ULLIA were asked to examine new models for providing reference services and, in particular, to consider how faculty librarians could be most strategically placed to support OSU's strategic goals. One of the major changes we needed to consider was whether or not a faculty librarian was needed at the reference desk to provide services. In the next section, I will describe the process used to engage library faculty in shaping the future of reference services at OSU Libraries.

OSU Libraries, like many other academic libraries, recorded a decline in the number of reference questions asked at the physical reference desk.[1] Between 2003 and 2006, reference questions dropped 53 percent and we began questioning the value of having our most expensive resource, faculty librarians, tethered to a reference desk "just in case" a reference question was asked.

In 2006, OSU Libraries departments were defining goals based on a new strategic plan, adopted in 2004. This new plan recognized that the information landscape had tipped from print to an increased emphasis and reliance on digital resources. In order for us to move this strategic plan forward, OSU library faculty members would be required to partner with academic departments in new ways to enhance student learning and faculty research and to communicate, educate, and bridge issues of scholarly communication, data management, and digitized collections. On the collections side, OSU librarians were increasingly focused on developing and showcasing not only our own unique collections, but also student and faculty research. In Reference and Instruction, we recognized that we needed to develop tools and services that would enable the student and faculty community to successfully navigate and discover digital resources, and to work effectively in this new environment.

Creating new faculty librarian positions was not an option in an already economically strapped state university. To deal with this, and with the changing nature of research and teaching needs on our campus, OSU Libraries underwent a succession of reorganizations between 2006 and 2009, the most significant in 2009.[2] To ensure that our services and resources were aligned with the university's mission, and that we used our limited number of library faculty effectively, the library administration and departmental managers engaged in conversations to determine what types of departments, units, and individual librarian positions were needed to move our strategic plan forward.

By 2008, the process of reorganization and strategic planning had made it clear that significant changes were coming for reference services we provided and rethinking our reference collections in the digital environment and developing new services designed to increase student academic success. To meet our goals, reference and instruction librarians were needed to work on strategic projects and new initiatives. With the strong support of the University Librarian, reference and instruction librarians developed a plan that would result in the removal of full-time library faculty from the physical reference desk and the integration of the print reference collection into the circulating collection.

Integration of the Reference Collections

Enrollment at OSU has increased steadily since the late 1990s, jumping from 16,061 in 1999 to 22,000 students in 2008. Not surprisingly, this increase in population brought with it an increased demand for library study spaces. In 2008, in alignment with our strategic plan, many of our print subscriptions had been replaced by electronic collections. Our usage statistics showed a decline in the use of the print reference collections and anecdotal evidence suggested that the library faculty and library users were more likely to look up information online than utilize the paper reference collections. In 2008, the reference collection measured 5,040 linear feet. A portion of our most expensive collections sat fallow on the shelf and prime library real estate on the main floor of the library was being used as a storage space for an unused collection.

In the spring of 2008, faculty librarians in Research and Innovative Services, Undergraduate Learning and Library Access Services and Collection Services made the bold decision to integrate the reference collection into the circulation stacks. This move was inspired by a bigger project that involved the first phase of transforming the Information Commons built in 1999 into a Learning Commons. One goal was to open up and refurnish the space to accommodate the increasingly collaborative nature of student learning needs. The first phase of the reference weeding project was very conservative and involved moving approximately 14 percent of the reference collection into the circulating stacks. In this phase, faculty librarians concentrated mainly on the huge runs of paper indexes that had been replaced by electronic resources, withdrawing content that was duplicated electronically and moving the back sets of indexes to storage. They also made the decision to move everything they considered nonessential for reference to the circulating stacks.

In the second phase of the reference process, one faculty member in the Collections department reviewed the entire reference collection title by title and gathered recommendations from library subject specialists about individual titles. Subject specialists indicated whether a title should move to the circulating collection, move to storage, or be withdrawn from the collection. Most of the items that moved to the stacks circulate for one week. There are fifty titles in the circulating collections that are library use only. These are specialized subject indexes for which OSU Libraries has no digital versions, foreign language dictionaries, assorted field guides, engineering standards, and handbooks.

Once those decisions had been made, staff and students from the Cataloging and Collection Maintenance departments developed processes and procedures for relocating the materials and updating the status of the titles in the online catalog. Most of this work was done over the summer, when many of our users are away from campus. Users on campus were kept informed by signage in the Learning Commons near where the reference collection resided, and by several e-mail messages to OSU academic departments and advisors. We also made sure that library staff, particularly those at our public service desks, were up-to-date with the reference collection move so they could assist library users as needed.

We anticipated that when the term resumed in the fall, returning faculty and students would find the lack of a reference collection disruptive. Over the ten-week term we tracked any questions regarding the reference collection at the reference desk. To our surprise, we had very few inquiries about why the reference collection had moved. The collection move went virtually unnoticed by the OSU community.

The reaction from library faculty was similarly muted. Several reference librarians commented that it was not as convenient for them to use their favorite print reference sources now that they had been relocated, but no other substantial comments were received. However, library staff members in collection maintenance and cataloging expressed concerns we had not anticipated. These staff members were very uncomfortable with the faculty librarians' decision to relocate the reference collection in the circulating collection. The staff were concerned that library faculty had not engaged in a deliberate, informed process before making the decision to eliminate parts of the reference collection that we had digital access to and relocate the remainder of the collection. To address staff concerns, the Head of Collections engaged staff from circulation, collection maintenance and cataloging in a discussion that elaborated on the vision, planning, and process that was developed to eliminate a separate reference collection at OSU Libraries.

Our process might have gone a bit smoother if we had spent more time up front discussing the rationale for our decision and educating staff on current collection trends before we began the process.

One of our goals in this process was to increase circulation of an underutilized collection; between November 2009 and May 2011, 282 former reference titles had circulated. As a result of this move, OSU Libraries no longer has a separate collection fund for reference titles and has shifted our reference collection priorities to an increased focus on providing access to information on mobile devices, and providing digital content in any format the future brings us.

Developing a New Reference Service Model

Like most librarians, we began by conducting a literature search to identify different models for providing academic library reference desk staffing and services. We did not find a definitive consensus, and realized that while there are similarities between academic library reference services, every institution is unique. However, from the literature, we identified a number of methodologies that we employed to help us make our decision. We used a variety of data points to gather information for our project. These included:

- analyzing our own reference statistics
- tracking all questions asked at the desk during a specific time period
- ranking desk questions as: must be answered by a reference librarian; information; and technical
- conducting focus groups to get information from reference service providers
- conducting a user satisfaction survey
- analyzing the peak busy times in the Learning Commons and drawing connections between user traffic and the amount of staffing needed at the desk
- surveying part-time reference librarians about their availability and ability to provide service at our reference desk

The analysis of our usage statics showed that, similar to other academic libraries, we have experienced a drop in the number of reference questions being asked over time. From 2003 to 2008 we saw a 53 percent decline in

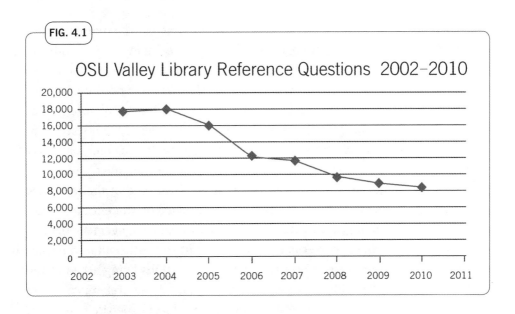

FIG. 4.1

OSU Valley Library Reference Questions 2002–2010

in-person questions asked at the reference desk. During this time period we adjusted our staffing levels at the reference desk a number of times in response to the decline in reference transactions. However, our reference desk model continued to rely on the physical presence of at least one faculty librarian at the reference desk between the hours of 9:00 a.m. and 9:00 p.m. Monday through Thursday; 9:00 a.m. and 6:00 p.m. Friday; 10:00 a.m. and 6:00 p.m. Saturday; and 10:00 a.m. and 10:00 p.m. Sunday (see figure 4.1.)

In order to change our model we needed to tackle the assumption that a faculty librarian needs to be physically present at the desk in order for reference services to be provided adequately. Our literature search had uncovered a number of studies that looked at the cost effectiveness of staffing the desk with faculty librarians. Susan Ryan of Stetson University in Florida presented a good overview of a methodology her institution used to calculate the cost effectiveness of using library faculty at their reference service desk. Stetson concluded that it was not cost effective to use faculty librarians at the desk and that staffing models should be examined more closely.[3] One similarity among the cost effectiveness studies we examined in our literature review was that each institution logged reference transactions over a specific period of time and then performed an analysis on the type of question being asked to determine if the question needed a librarian to answer it. We decided to replicate this measure at a smaller scale to benchmark our institution with others in the study.

In November of 2008, we logged every question asked at the reference desk for ten days during a high library use period that coincided with midterm examinations on campus. Reference desk staff coded questions as Reference, Directional, or Technical and then each transaction was reviewed by a senior library faculty member. This faculty member, who had more than ten years of experience in reference services at OSU Libraries, ranked the questions to determine if they required the expertise of a library faculty member, or if they could be answered by a well-trained reference desk staff member. Like other studies, ours found that the majority of the questions asked at the reference desk could be answered by a well-trained library staff or student employee. After the initial ranking, the Head of the Teaching and Engagement department analyzed the question set and concluded that staff other than a library faculty member could answer 80 percent of the questions being asked at the reference desk. Of the 272 questions that had been tagged "reference," only 11 percent required a library faculty member with subject expertise to answer. The largest number of questions asked at the reference desk were for "known items," materials OSU Libraries owned, followed by a category of questions that the department head labeled "Tier 1 Reference," questions that could be answered quickly by checking an online or web resource. The majority of the Tier 1 questions were some form of "how do I get started finding information on a particular subject" and could be handled by staff, students, or part-time librarians.

An infrastructure was already in place to handle those questions that did require subject expertise. In 1999, OSU Libraries had embraced a reference model that was similar to the Brandeis model.[4] Under this model, the reference desk became a reference/information desk staffed with a reference librarian, a classified employee, and a student assistant. Any questions that took over 15 minutes to answer were referred to a subject specialist for research consultation follow-up, either in person, by phone, or e-mail. Our scheduled reference desk staff and student employees were trained and accustomed to assisting library users to begin a general subject information search using an aggregated subject database such as EBSCO*host*'s Academic Search Premier, the OSU Libraries online catalog, or other search engines to locate materials.

The third largest category of questions asked at the reference desk focused on other library services and how to use those services to access information effectively. Again, our expectation was that anyone working at the reference desk was trained to be familiar with our library services, resource sharing tools, and other online services to assist library users both face-to-face or virtually (see figure 4.2).

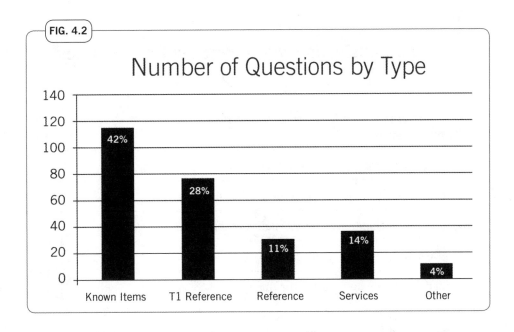

FIG. 4.2

Number of Questions by Type

- Known Items: 42%
- T1 Reference: 28%
- Reference: 11%
- Services: 14%
- Other: 4%

We recognized that changes to our reference services staff model would also impact our library users. In collaboration with our Research and Innovative Services department, we designed a survey to obtain feedback from the individuals who utilized the reference services (see figure 4.3). We received thirty-one responses and they all indicated (1) that they received the help they needed from the reference desk; (2) that they would come back to the desk for assistance; and (3) that they were treated with courtesy and respect. We also asked the respondents if they would be willing to wait for an answer via referral. Twenty-five indicated they would be willing to wait, two were undecided, and four respondents said they would not wait. Unfortunately, the survey was conducted during our summer session and the response rate was very low.

Focus Groups

The reference service task force realized that it was critical to involve the individuals responsible for providing reference services at the desk in the planning process. We needed their buy-in for the venture, and we wanted to acknowledge their expertise. We also wanted to use that expertise to help determine if a library faculty member was essential at the reference desk. We conducted a series of four focus groups targeting the four types of staff who provided reference services at the desk: library faculty, on-call librarians, paraprofessionals, and student employees. Our first focus group was with the faculty librarians who staffed the desk.

FIG. 4.3

User Satisfaction with Reference Desk Services

Tell us about your experience at this desk today!

Based only on your experience today, please answer the following questions:	Yes	No	Not sure
Did you get the help or answer you hoped for?			
Would you come back to this desk for additional assistance?			
Would you be willing to wait for assistance at this desk?			
I was treated with respect and courtesy.			
I learned something about using the library.			

I came to this desk today because for this/these reasons: (check as many as apply):

- ☐ Laptop printing or color printer use
- ☐ Computer problem
- ☐ Building directions
- ☐ Help with use of library website
- ☐ Help with locating an item
- ☐ Help with locating information on a topic or for a class assignment.
- ☐ Other: _____

Please circle your OSU affiliation | Undergrad   Grad   Student   Faculty   Staff   Other

When completed, please leave this survey in one of the collection boxes. Thank you!

As with academic librarians throughout the nation, our public service librarians considered reference services one of their core professional functions; they assumed oversight and responsibility for providing reference services and research consultations at OSU Libraries. Knowing this, we wanted to know from the library faculty perspective not only what services and expectations our library users had when they came to the reference desk, but how librarians viewed their own role in the reference desk. Finally, we wanted their thoughts on what they could give up doing at the reference desk.

Two themes emerged from the faculty librarian focus group. The first theme focused on the library user experience. Faculty librarians perceived that library patrons wanted their questions answered quickly in a safe, non-threatening environment. When asked their current roles at the reference desk, library faculty indicated they were at the desk to make sure that library users feel comfortable asking questions, to provide oversight and responsibility for developing the services being offered and for the quality of service library users received at the reference desk.

When asked what they could give up at the reference desk, the librarians indicated that they were ready to give up the day-to-day oversight of operations at the desk and, most importantly, that they could give up answering known-item, informational, or directional questions. This raised the question of referrals. We asked the library faculty for their preferences about how reference questions should be referred to them. Most of them indicated that there should be some level of triage done to weed out informational questions, general subject database questions, and known-item searching. The librarians' responses seemed to indicate they cared about the quality and service that was being offered and the library user experience, but did not necessarily see a need to staff the reference desk.

Our next series of focus groups were with part-time librarians, staff, and students who provide services at the reference desk. We started each focus group with the premise that library faculty would no longer staff the physical reference desk and we asked a series of six questions that examined what role each type of service provider played at the desk. We also asked for their perceptions about library users and their expectations. We shifted the focus of the questions we asked the library faculty slightly so that we could get more specific information back from the students, staff, and part-time librarians to address how staff were currently referring reference questions to library faculty, and what type of a referral process they thought should be in place if there were no faculty librarians staffing the reference desk. Finally we asked these groups to describe the training and support they would need if we pursued a model that did not include library faculty staffing the reference desk.

In answer to the first two questions, the part-time librarians and paraprofessional staff agreed with the library faculty focus group that library users wanted a comfortable, welcoming place where they could ask any question, and that users expected answers when they came to the desk. Additionally, our part-time librarians and student employees indicated that library users were not interested in instruction but usually just wanted an answer. They also suggested that users were not receptive to having to wait for an answer if the question was referred to a subject expert: "[t]hey want service and they want it fast."

While all three focus groups agreed in theory that a library faculty member did not need to be physically present at the reference desk in order for reference service to be provided, faculty librarians felt strongly that they should continue providing in-depth reference consultations and they expressed deep concern about the need for desk staff to refer those questions. There was also a clear consensus from the faculty librarians that they were responsible for the quality and level of service provided at the reference desk, even if they did not physically staff that desk. Our students, staff, and part-time librarians who staffed the desk were open to the idea of referring questions to faculty librarians but wanted to be sure that they received appropriate additional training and had access to library faculty support when needed.

These concerns stemmed from the need for effective communication between faculty librarians and reference desk staff. Desk staff needed clear mechanisms to effectively and efficiently refer patron questions to subject specialists.

Related to this, faculty librarians and reference staff were exploring online tools and services that would enable users to contact us without having to be physically present in the library. With faculty and staff concerns about effective communication and our desire to extend our virtual reference services in mind, we identified two new online services to launch Fall Term 2009. First, we adopted an online chat service that allowed all reference services staff to log in to the service simultaneously and transfer chat sessions among logged in users. We also invested in a text service that enabled our users to contact us with their mobile devices.

The other concern that we needed to address before we could propose a new service model for reference related to the level of service provided. Faculty librarians felt they were ultimately responsible for the quality of the service provided, so they needed a way to stay connected to the services provided at the desk. At the same time, the students and part-time librarians who would be staffing the desk needed a "safety net" that would allow them to get immediate help when they needed it. Faculty librarians decided that for at least the first year of the new service model they would provide support to the desk staff virtually, using the new chat service.

To address the training needs for the desk staff, a small group of library faculty analyzed the questions logged from the reference desk transaction survey conducted to identify the types of questions that part-time librarians, paraprofessional staff, and students could expect to answer at the reference desk. The same small group developed a series of training modules that provided training on resources to answer questions asked at the desk and on using the tools and technology needed as well as behavioral training that covered the basics of how to conduct a "reference interview," and when to refer a question to a library faculty member. Training materials included training plans and online tutorials for:

- Conducting a Reference Interview Tutorial
- Library Website Tutorial
- Known-item Search Tutorial
- Journal Search Tutorial

The referral process was another area of concern for both library faculty and desk staff. To address this concern we developed a robust referral process grounded in our commitment to providing superior service to our library user. First, we set a clear service expectation for all service providers at the reference desk: no library user was to be turned away from our service desk without receiving an answer, a referral, or a set of resources to examine. Second, we established a clear delineation of responsibility and communicated it to all service providers at the desk: referrals are the responsibility of library employees, NOT the library user (see figure 4.4).

Finally, to directly address the concern from library faculty to ensure that the service levels at the reference desk remained consistent and there was direct oversight of the services, we repurposed our library instruction coordinator position to a Learning Commons coordinator position. The duties of this position involve daily supervision of the staff and oversight of day-to-day operations of the reference desk.

Summary

In the fall of 2009, we implemented the new model, with no faculty librarians staffing the reference desk in the Commons. The reference desk is now labeled the information desk and is staffed by a pool of part-time librarians, student assistants, one paraprofessional staff member and the Learning Commons coordinator. Library faculty are available for research consultation by request and provide backup reference support to the information desk virtually and by chat. We are still in the process of analyzing how successful our new service model has been, but anecdotally we can relate that library staff and users have been happy with the arrangement.

In the future, our intent is to conduct an analysis of transcripts of the virtual reference services that the library provides to determine if the types of questions that faculty are answering through the chat and e-mail reference are similar to the questions being asked of the staff at the physical desk. If we find that the questions and ratio of questions being asked virtually are in alignment with what the desk staff is currently doing, we will look to release

---

FIG. 4.4

Referral Process

When you are unable to answer a patron's inquiry, you will confer with other employees including other student employees, library staff, and librarians. Under no circumstances is a patron to be turned away without answering the inquiry, referring the inquiry, or providing the patron with sources to consult for more information.

Referrals are the responsibility of library employees, NOT the patron. Handing business cards to patrons as a referral mechanism will occur ONLY if the patron specifically requests it.

Specific Referral Processes

Weekdays 7:30 a.m.–10:00 a.m.; Fridays 5:00 p.m.–8:00 p.m.;
Saturdays and Sundays 10:00 a.m.–1:00 p.m.

- As the Information Desk is staffed only by student employees, questions that cannot be answered at the Information Desk must be referred using the online Reference Referral Form.
- These referrals are answered by faculty librarians after 10:00 a.m. Monday through Friday.

Weekdays 10:00 a.m.–5:00 p.m.

- Student employees will refer questions to the part-time librarian (PTL). If the PTL is busy, student employees can refer using LibraryH3lp.
- The faculty librarian covering LibraryH3lp is the "generalist/specialist" serving as backup and is responsible for answering the more complex questions that come to the Information Desk.
- Use LibraryH3lp to contact the backup/chat librarian to let her know you have a patron at the Desk who needs in-depth assistance.
- The backup/chat librarian will determine how to answer the question. She can answer the question through chat, can meet with the patron at the Information Desk or can ask that the question be referred using the online Reference Referral Form.
- If the backup/chat librarian decides to answer the question via chat, direct the patron to use the Consultation Station computer. At this point, all remaining contact is between the backup/chat librarian.

Sunday–Thursday 5:00 p.m.–1:00 a.m.

- Student employees will refer questions they cannot answer to other Information Desk staff (PTL 5:00–9:00 p.m., Night Library Tech. II, 9:00 p.m.–1:00 a.m.).

faculty from their virtual reference service duties. More importantly, we need to conduct another library user satisfaction survey. In the next survey, we want to move beyond satisfaction with the reference services we are providing and focus on our library users' academic success. We want to identify other services and resources we should be offering that will further strengthen their success. Finally, as library faculty are released from additional reference services, OSU Libraries continues to investigate what is the best use of library faculty time and where will these library faculty have the biggest impact on the learning outcomes and research mission of Oregon State University.

Bookend

IN THE INTRODUCTION to this case study, we used the phrase "magical thinking," and stated that we need to move beyond the magic to critically assess our services. Cheryl Middleton gave us one clear-headed way to examine reference services.

But in his 2012 book *The 7 Laws of Magical Thinking*, Matthew Hutson makes it clear that we all use and need a bit of magic to stay sane and to go on working in our increasingly hectic lives. Sometimes, the magical thinking can be beneficial, giving us a sense of control and power over uncertain situations. But any time we succumb to thoughts of luck or destiny or "it was all meant to be," we're engaging in magical thinking.[5] If we knock on wood, cross our fingers for luck, or think that we really can control the outcome of a Pittsburgh Steelers game by yelling at the TV, we're thinking magically. If we believe that some legacy library services are so vital that they will never change, guess what? We're engaging in our own library magic.

Magical thinking is also related to a kind of fetishization of the profession and the tools of our profession. Kathleen Fitzpatrick writes of the "undead" academic press book—haunting us all from beyond the grave in a zombie state of monographic scholarship. Fitzpatrick doesn't really believe the that academic publishing is ready for the grave, but she does urge us to think beyond our singular, magical focus on print, and open up to new ways of scholarly discourse.[6] In the same way, librarians and those that love libraries can step aside and start to recognize library services that, like zombies, are no longer viable. Fetishizing objects, ideas, and services is a classic case of magical thinking in action.

But is some of our "magical thinking" really all that magical, or is it, as Daniel Kahneman attests, a form of expert intuition?[7] In his award-winning book, *Thinking, Fast and Slow*, Kahneman relates the story of seasoned chess players who, after years of play, simply see the chessboard differently than the rest of us. With a glance at a game in play, a chess master can see several winning moves. The expertise is gained through thousands of hours of play and study, and results in a predictable level of expertise. In the same way, library changes may be painfully obvious if we allow ourselves to see them. Those of us with years of experience can walk into a library and immediately start to evaluate service points and public spaces. We can identify issues at a glance, and should recognize when our expert intuition is a valid starting point for further research. We might even, like Fitzpatrick, be able to quickly identify some zombies: practices that are no longer viable, yet still seemingly required in our libraries. This kind of "fast thinking" and evaluation should not, however, fall prey to the danger of fast solutions; Kahneman makes it clear that we often ignore what we don't know and shouldn't trust subjective confidence. Even if we are experts, we might not know the limits of our expertise.[8]

This is why case studies and research and data are so vital to our processes. Even if we know, or think we know, the solution to our problems, we need the means to make the best decisions possible for our institutions. Having the data and making the process transparent will also be invaluable in trying to sell solutions to your stakeholders. It's a process of self-mediation essential to our survival.

REFERENCES

1. Charles Martell, "The Absent User: Physical Use of Academic Library Collections and Services Continues to Decline 1995–2006," *Journal of Academic Librarianship* 34, no. 5 (2008): 400–407.

2. Jennifer E. Nutefall and Faye A. Chadwell, "Preparing for the 21st Century: Academic Library Realignment," *New Library World* 113, no. 3/4 (2012): 162–173.

3. Susan M. Ryan, "Reference Transactions Analysis: The Cost-Effectiveness of Staffing Traditional Academic Reference Desk," *The Journal of Academic Librarianship* 34, no. 5 (2008): 289–299.

4. Virginia Massey-Burzio, "Reference Encounters of a Different Kind: A Sympsium," *Journal of Academic Librarianship* 18, no. 5 (1992): 276–286.

5. Matthew Hutson, *The 7 Laws of Magical Thinking: How Irrational Beliefs Keep Us Happy, Healthy, and Sane* (New York: Hudson Street Press, 2012), 2.

6. Kathleen Fitzpatrick, *Planned Obsolescence: Publishing, Technology, and the Future of the Academy* (New York: NYU Press, 2011), 4–5.

7. Daniel Kahneman, *Thinking, Fast and Slow* (New York: Farrar, Straus and Giroux, 2011), 12.

8. Ibid, 240.

University of California, Santa Cruz

IN THIS COAUTHORED case study, we see how the University of California Santa Cruz's librarians identify themselves as service providers, and how their ability to provide service is shaken by a series of budget cuts. Following the adage of "never waste a good crisis," the librarians take us through a six-year process of redefining how and where public service takes place in their renovated institution. With the clear goal of always providing better service, the librarians' focus on core values and goals carried them through what they hope will be the worst crisis they'll ever face.

The "never waste a good crisis" phrase has recently been used by current Chicago mayor Rahm Emanuel to describe issues facing President Obama's administration. In 2009, Emanuel framed the economic downturn as an opportunity "to do things you think you could not do before." But according to the *Yale Book of Quotations* editor Fred Shapiro, the "crisis" phrase dates back to a 1976 article in the journal *Medical Economics* by M. F. Weiner entitled "Don't Waste a Crisis—Your Patient's or Your Own." Almost forty years ago, Weiner urged patients and physicians to use a medical crisis to improve all parts of a person's lifestyle.[1]

But do we have the ability and foresight, in the midst of a crisis, to understand what's going on and to proactively react? Like others in this book, librarians at UC Santa Cruz were faced with a massive crisis that was beyond their control. The way they prepared for, worked through, and communicated change in their libraries was key to finding solutions to their problems.

A Good Crisis

Reinventing Critical Services

Greg Careaga, M. Elizabeth Cowell, Nicole Lawson, Lucia Orlando, and Sarah Troy

FOR A GENERATION, the organizational identity of the UC Santa Cruz (UCSC) Library was defined by one word: service. Of the eight mature general campuses of the University of California (UC), ours was the only one with a library that was not a member of the Association of Research Libraries. We made up for our smaller collection size by the quality of service we provided, and the depth of the relationships we formed with our students and faculty.

In recent years, two factors combined that challenged us to reexamine our approach. We temporarily closed the largest campus library for a major renovation and moved operations into a new wing. Our budget—which had been in general but manageable decline—took the first of several major shocks as the university, state, and nation reacted to the largest economic contraction since the Great Depression.

From FY 2007–2011, the Library reinvented itself in several significant ways. We moved buildings twice. We reorganized twice. We cut and then restored hours. We recast our Access and Reference departments. We fundamentally changed every librarian's job.

Reflection and change have become part of our organizational culture. This case study will focus on one facet of the Library's transformation: our public services. Specifically, we will describe how we reorganized in response to budget cuts, identified and cut services for which the cost was out of proportion to the benefit, and substantially reinvented other services that were mission critical but inefficiently delivered.

FY 2007: Annus Commutatus

LEADERSHIP

We experienced major turnover in the leadership of our public services units this year. The acting head of Access Services transferred to Collection Development. Two new librarians were recruited to team lead Access Services. Our long-tenured and well-respected head of Reference retired and the Library recruited an Associate University Librarian (AUL) for Public Services, a new position in the Library.

MOVING HOUSE

Between 2005 and 2008, the McHenry Library Renovation and Addition Project completed a new 110,000-square-foot wing to the library. Our last, big challenge of the year would be to move 654,000 volumes and eighty-nine staff out of the existing 114,860 assignable square foot (ASF) building into the smaller 81,600 ASF addition, so that the old building could be seismically retrofitted and substantially renovated over the next 30 months. We accomplished the move over the course of a five-day Spring Break, and opened on March 31, 2008. Our staff performed brilliantly. By the end, they were also exhausted, uprooted from their routines and familiar surroundings, and more than a bit dazed.

New leadership and new facilities left us better positioned to effect large-scale transformational change than we had been in a generation.

FY 2008: Storm Clouds

On September 23, 2008, Governor Schwarzenegger signed the California State Budget for FY 2008–2009, 85 days after the start of the fiscal year. Even for a state accustomed to missing its statutory June 30 budget deadline, this one was historically late. It was also historically challenging for both K–12 and higher education. We knew this was a game changer. Fortunately, we saw it coming. The University, campus, and Library had prepared for the crisis, and that readiness bought us the time to make an orderly transition.

STRATEGIC PLANNING

We laid the foundation for transformation by performing an evaluation of our strategic priorities. Our process extended over five months, from August to December 2008, and involved a consultant, senior and middle managers, librarians, and staff. The work product influenced our organizational structure and gave us a metric for evaluating services. Subsequent discussions of adding, reconfiguring, or eliminating a service came back to the question of how a proposed change contributed to furthering the Library's strategic priorities. Likewise, as staff positions opened due to attrition, those positions dissociated from their host departments and reverted to the control of senior management. They were then either commended to the tender mercies of the budget axe, or—less frequently—reconstituted in support of the Library's most pressing needs. Senior management made a conscious choice to absorb cuts in our staffing levels through attrition rather than targeted layoffs, and attrition hit Access Services particularly hard in the years leading up to 2009. While the Library strives to time its biggest changes for the start of the fiscal year in July, a 5 percent midyear budget cut in FY 2008 and accompanying portents of doom for FY 2009 motivated us to get an early start.

SLUG EXPRESS

Slug Express, our document delivery service, was highly valued by a small group of faculty members, staff, and graduate students. The service allowed them to have books pulled from the stacks and sent to their campus offices. Print journal articles could also be scanned and sent electronically for a small fee. Our Interlibrary Loan (ILL) unit managed this service and processed approximately three thousand requests each year.

For a fairly straightforward service, Slug Express required a commitment of substantial staff and student employee resources to print new requests, pull items from the stacks, check them out via the ILS, and package them for delivery through campus mail. Campus Mail Services charged a per item fee for each package. Furthermore, various administrative complications demanded additional staff time for a fair number of these requests.

In the wake of a midyear cut, we decided that Slug Express did not merit its costs. The service was used by only a small population; it was expensive in terms of staff time, physical resources, and delivery costs, totaling $40,000 per year. The service ended on March 20, 2009.

Senior management was aware that this change would be unpopular. It was certain to be an unwelcome note in the tattoo of service cuts and cost increases that described life at UC in the wake of economic collapse. In an attempt to educate users about the decision, the AUL for Public Services and ILL staff created a Frequently Asked Questions page. The FAQ described the service, why it was ending, and the other options that patrons had available. The University Librarian drafted a letter that was sent to each of the heaviest Slug Express users in February 2009, explaining that the service was ending because of the deteriorating budget climate. Nearly 100 faculty and graduate student supporters signed a petition to the Campus Provost, Executive Vice Chancellor, and the University Librarian asking that we retain the service.

Many others e-mailed the Library directly. Despite the grassroots support, the service ended as planned.

RESEARCH SERVICES

Early public service changes were not limited to Access Services. Our Research Services department, the traditional bastion of our "high-touch" service model, also experienced diminishing resources and started the process of assessment and consolidation. At this early stage, the efficiencies were limited to eliminating double staffing at the McHenry reference desk during morning hours and weekends. In December of 2008, the AUL for Public Services decided that we would join the QuestionPoint chat reference service along with our sister UC campuses. This service gave our users access to chat reference service 24/7. Our initial contribution was a modest two hours per week.

FY 2009: Annus Horribilis

Hard on the heels of our 5 percent midyear cut in FY 2008, we absorbed an additional 18 percent permanent budget cut, did not fill ten vacancies that came open during the year, and had to initiate a campus-mandated, one-year variable furlough program for librarians and staff that created an additional 3 percent reduction in available human resources. We had long since exhausted the reservoir of easy fixes. The time had come for more drastic change.

HOURS

We substantially cut our hours. We reduced each building from 98 to 67 open hours per week during the academic calendar. To offset the impact of the cuts, we were able to offer extended hours during finals week, staying open until 3:00 a.m.

These cuts were unpopular. Our decision to close on Saturdays was particularly criticized, even though it was by far our lightest day for gate count. Our abbreviated schedule was one in a series of campus service curtailments that contributed to a climate of protest that year. Student disapprobation manifested in the occupation of several campus buildings. The Library was targeted for occupation twice. First, in an effort to keep the Library open on Saturdays, a group of up to 300 students and protesters occupied the Science and Engineering Library (S&E) on the afternoon of Friday, November 13, 2009, and remained in the building for approximately 24 hours. In May 2010, a group calling itself Students for the Library staged a three-day occupation that coincided with midterms, in an effort to force the Library to keep the S&E Library open until midnight.

FIRST REORGANIZATION

A major outcome of the previous year's strategic planning was a department-level reorganization of the Library that took effect with the advent of the new fiscal year in July 2009. Two new departments were created: Digital Initiatives, and Teaching and Learning Services. One department was eliminated: S&E. We did not close that library, but instead made a conscious decision to integrate duplicate circulation, collection maintenance, reserves (all Access Services units), and reference operations with their counterparts at McHenry Library.

With reduced staffing at each location, consolidation and cross-training between facilities had become essential. At the same time, we hoped to realize a change in the organizational culture and inculcate the meme of "two buildings, one Library" into the consciousness of our staff.

ACCESS SERVICES

The Access Services departments from the two campus libraries began meeting in May 2009 to discuss how to merge staff and services. Access Services looked different in each library. In McHenry Library, Circulation and Stacks was a single unit. McHenry also had a Reserves unit and housed the ILL unit. In S&E, there was no ILL counterpart, Stacks (known as Collection Maintenance) was separate from Circulation, and Circulation and Reserves was a single unit. How were we to reconcile such disparate models? It felt like we had to cut the Gordian Knot and start fresh. And that is what we did.

We leveraged the leaders within the units. We had three senior staff members with a wealth of experience in the areas of Circulation, Collection Maintenance, and Reserves. During a meeting of all affected staff, we invited a frank discussion about which unit they would most like to work in given their interests and skills. Staff working in ILL have a specialized set of skills and are classified at a higher level, so they were exempt from this process. Remaining staff sorted themselves out among the remaining units: Circulation, Collection Maintenance, and Reserves.

When the Access Services merger went live on July 1, there was resistance on the part of some. Staff began working public service desk shifts in both libraries. Working in a new desk environment required an adjustment period. When we had moments of doubt, we reviewed our stated goals to bring us back on track.

Our primary goal was to provide better service. Prior to the merger, policies were applied inconsistently between buildings. Patrons might get completely different answers to the same questions depending on which library's service desk they asked. Second, we wanted to create a more flexible workforce. The more knowledge we shared between units, the better service we could provide, and the more useful we could be to other units when their workloads increased. The new structure also created a larger pool of desk workers to pull from when someone got sick or took a vacation. Merging units also allowed us to streamline our processes to make them more efficient. We often found that one desk had been handling things in a way that made much better sense, and, when that happened, we adopted that method for both desks. Over time, as everyone saw that the best ideas prevailed, negative feelings over change subsided.

> We often found that one desk had been handling things in a way that made much better sense, and, when that happened, we adopted that method for both desks.

PROFESSIONAL STAFF

Even before the budget crisis, the Library saw its cohort of librarians diminish over time. Our student-to-librarian ratio increased from 436 students to 1 librarian in FY 2001 to 760 students to 1 librarian in FY 2009 due to attrition in our professional ranks and increasing enrollment. As our colleagues left, our bibliographers had to take on more subject assignments. Our reference librarians were also called upon to assume some collections responsibilities. Our teaching load for lower division general research skills instruction was keeping pace with increasing enrollments. At the same time, our reference desk traffic had been in steady decline for years. The reference desk was an obvious albeit unpopular place to look for greater efficiencies.

RESEARCH SERVICES

We made significant changes in 2009 to our reference staffing models at both libraries. We reduced the McHenry reference desk service from 64 to 55 hours per week. We eliminated double staffing in favor of a backup model for busy hours, and thereby reduced our weekly commitment of librarian time on the desk from 89 hours to between 55 and 75 hours. We eliminated the Reference Aides program, a volunteer service open to library assistants from other departments, thus saving another 20 hours per week of library staff time. We maintained Sunday and evening reference service.

We also reduced service at the S&E reference desk from 56 to 35 hours. That desk was supported by a smaller cadre of librarians and didn't have a tradition of double staffing. Neither did it have a Reference Aides program. We decided to eliminate evening and weekend reference service at S&E.

UC increased its commitment to the QuestionPoint consortium and in Winter Quarter, our local obligation to support the service increased from 2 to 9 hours per week.

FY 2010: Reprieve

MEASURE 42

The greatly reduced service profile of 2009 took a toll on the Library and campus. Our students needed late-night access to our facilities and collections, and we had failed them. Without a new source of funding, we could not reinstate library hours. Fortunately, some highly committed students helped us work with the Student Union Assembly (SUA) to conceive and pass Measure 42, a referendum that levied a small fee on students to restore our hours to FY08 levels for three years. The decentralized nature of student government made garnering support across campus difficult. Fortunately, our students lobbied hard and the referendum passed with over 80 percent of the vote. As a result, we hired four part-time, temporary library assistants and increased our pool of student library assistants in time to restore hours for the start of the 2010–11 academic year.

RESEARCH SERVICES

We didn't implement big changes to our reference desk staffing model in FY10. We dropped backup staffing for the McHenry desk, and notwithstanding the fact that the Library had restored open hours on Saturdays, we did not restore Saturday reference service.

We knew that future budget cuts might affect reference service and undertook an effort to automate and enrich our data gathering for reference transactions. We used SurveyMonkey to gather the usual data of transaction duration and time of day. We also collected brief narrative data in order to distinguish between those reference interviews that required a librarian's professional skill and those that did not.

SHARED SERVICE POINT WORKING GROUP

We began preparing for the new McHenry public service desk early in Fall Quarter the year before we moved into the renovated space. Offering Access and Reference support from a shared service desk near the main entrance was an important part of our plan for the renovation. Our looming deadline proved to be an effective goad that motivated us to resolve the details of harmonizing the practices of the Reference and Access Services desks. We recognized that a top-down approach would not effectively achieve our goal of a coordinated service point, and so we prevailed upon staff across all public services departments to participate and to bring their best thinking and cooperative efforts to the task.

The meta-group, named the Shared Service Point Working Group (SSPWG), was composed of three subordinate groups, and those were subdivided into distinct functional areas. Each group reported to one of the Access Services or Research Services heads. They met regularly to coordinate responses to overlapping issues and provide consistent direction.

The Scheduling and Training Working Group developed scheduling guidelines for the new model and developed recommendations for methods and logistics pertaining to training staff to work at the desk. The Patron Service Standards Working Group developed the service standards expected from all public services staff. Finally, the Shared Work and Referrals Working Group developed a set of competencies and training checklists that formed the basis of the cross-training expectations for Research Services and Access Services staff at the colocated desks. This group also developed a set of referral guidelines for Access Services staff to assist them with referring questions to specialists.

Each group drafted reports articulating policy plans and guidelines, which were shared with all library staff members. The heads of Research Services, Access Services, and senior management reviewed each planning document and offered guidance and feedback to ensure the recommendations aligned with the Library's strategic directions.

ECOMMONS

The campus needed to replace its obsolete learning management system (LMS) and settled on the open-source Sakai platform as a successor. The Library was an essential partner in selecting and configuring our new "eCommons" system. We influenced local customization; specifically, we negotiated a separate "Reserves Manager" role that facilitated library access to each course's

"Resources" folder. We also improved copyright compliance controls. The Library had long used Docutek's ERes platform for managing electronic reserves. Some faculty members used this service; others used a variety of alternatives, sanctioned and otherwise. Our initial goal for a new LMS was for a system that would move us closer to offering students a single point of access for electronic reserves. Over time, our goal became to transition electronic reserves from a library-mediated service to one that was largely faculty managed.

We worked with the Faculty Instructional Technology Center to train and support faculty in the new paradigm, and by year's end we had effected a successful transition. There was one facet of electronic reserves that presented technical barriers to faculty self-service. The Library continues to process files for the more-technical streaming music reserves program. Once the eCommons structure was in place, the Library decommissioned ERes.

FY 2011: Reorganization Redux

The final reorganization to date went into effect in July 2011. It was partly driven by the conclusion of a decade-long McHenry Library Addition and Renovation Project. We finally got to move into our permanent spaces, which included our new combined service desk, substantial new public spaces, new staff spaces, and McHenry Library's new café. The reorganization was also informed by continued budget cuts, staff attrition, and the departure of one of the two heads of Access Services. To acknowledge the cross-departmental nature of our services, we implemented a team structure. The Public Services Team, made up of all staff that provide public service, met quarterly to review public service statistics, discuss issues with our merged services, and make plans for the coming quarter.

RESEARCH, INSTRUCTION, COLLECTIONS (RIC)

The Library had been adapting its professional staffing model away from specialization and toward generalization, as more librarians retired and were not replaced, and as budgets continued to deteriorate. Senior management decided that this was the proper time to complete the move to a "Research, Instruction, Collections" (RIC) model, with a formal matrix of librarian service expectations that described their responsibilities across these pillars of professional practice.

COLLECTION DEVELOPMENT

We maintained a core Collection Development department, but its focus shifted to managing consortial partnerships, approval plans, license agreements, and overseeing the collections budget and annual collections cycle. Much of the subject-level selection was apportioned to librarians in other departments, like Digital Initiatives and the newly constituted Research, Outreach and Instruction (ROI) department.

RESEARCH, OUTREACH AND INSTRUCTION (ROI)

The former Research Services and Teaching and Learning Services departments were combined to form ROI. Librarians in this department managed reference service (physical and virtual), Government Publications, bibliographic instruction, and nonsubject-specific outreach. Its librarians were given new collection assignments and the department assumed responsibility for training librarians from other departments in our instruction pedagogy.

This was a transformative year for reference service. With remaining librarians taking on so many new duties, we had to focus on how to reduce reference desk hours and still meet the needs of our campus constituents. In the months leading up to the transition, the Head of Research Services worked with the AUL for Public Services to analyze the data we had collected that year. SurveyMonkey's built-in tools allowed us to identify the busiest times of the day and provided a breakdown of the types of questions asked over the course of a quarter. We discovered the busiest times of day were different at each library. McHenry's heaviest traffic fell in the afternoon, but S&E was busiest in the late morning and early afternoon. We decided to stagger our reference hours between libraries, thereby expanding the times students could receive help from a librarian.

We also analyzed the narrative data to assess the level of knowledge required to answer different types of questions. Our analysis showed that a plurality of questions fell in the short category of 1 to 5 minutes and were of an informational rather than research nature. We determined that well-trained library assistants could handle these questions when a librarian was not present. We decided that each reference desk would be staffed 20 hours a week, 10 hours by a librarian and 10 hours by a high-level library assistant. We also decided to promote the availability of QuestionPoint during hours the desk was not staffed.

USER SERVICES AND RESOURCE SHARING (US&RS)

Prior to July 2011, User Services and Resource Sharing had been the two units that comprised Access Services. The Head of User Services departed in the spring and the Library decided not to fill her position. Instead, the Head of Resource Sharing was given the additional responsibility of managing User Services, and the new department US&RS (User Services and Resource Sharing) was thus created. This crew had long been the vanguard of our public service mission. Now that the new McHenry Library was set to open, they were about to take responsibility for servicing the largest building on campus. In a normal budget year we would have bolstered the department with increased staff. This year, as we strove to absorb new cuts and still avoid layoffs, we didn't have that luxury. We had to redeploy resources and cut services.

The Library decided to cut most preservation activities, moving this staff into the Collection Maintenance unit of US&RS. We also moved the Media Center out of Teaching and Learning Services and into the US&RS department. Finally, we created a new unit, Information Services, to manage the logistics of research service at the two libraries. This unit was staffed by two of our most senior library assistants, each of whom had many years of reference experience. They would also cover a plurality of reference desk service hours, giving oversubscribed librarians needed relief.

GROUP STUDY ROOMS

For 20 years, the Library had provided students with a suite of eight group-study rooms in S&E. We used our ILS to manage room access. We created records for the rooms and attached bar codes to key fobs. We took reservations, circulated keys, and assessed fines as necessary. It worked well for students and it worked well enough for library staff. But with a slew of new study rooms coming online in the renovated McHenry Library, we knew that we needed a more efficient, less labor-intensive solution.

The Library selected a proprietary system called LibCal. It adeptly manages access and does a good job enforcing our policies. It has allowed us to successfully replace a twenty-year-old, staff-intensive service that supported eight study rooms with an automated, mostly self-service model that supports forty-seven rooms. Based on one quarter's observations and applying very conservative metrics, we estimate that LibCal saves us 35 hours of staff desk time per week.

ROVING INFORMATION STUDENTS

The renovated McHenry Library has been very popular. Our gate counts this first year are double what they were during the construction years. In an effort to promote a safe and welcoming environment, we have implemented a Roving Information Program at both locations, reporting to the Information Services Unit. We trained students to answer basic research questions and deployed them where our users study in the buildings. These students act as eyes and ears for the staff, report anything out of the ordinary, facilitate the use of the group study rooms, and answer simple questions at the point of need. The service began in the fall of 2011 and is off to a good start. We provide this service 20 hours per week and hope to expand it.

FY 2012: Annus Incognitus

We are submitting this case study in the first days of a new fiscal year. We have a state budget that is not as bad as we feared it might be, but it is predicated on the success of Governor Brown's November ballot initiative to raise additional temporary revenues. While the Library and Campus are committed to maintaining service hours in FY 2013 when the student Measure 42 supplement expires, our ability to do so depends on the wisdom of California voters and the continued economic recovery. We shall have to wait and see.

Conclusion

Over a three-year period, the Library experienced a 31 percent permanent budget reduction and a 17 percent permanent reduction in staffing, while increasing the size of our physical plant by 42 percent. We could not have managed these difficult years under the old paradigm. While it wasn't easy to effect such massive change, we were ultimately successful. Our recent experience has taught us a lot about streamlining operations and recasting critical services to align with available resources. We are more agile now; our professional and support staffs have broader skill sets. We are more attuned to opportunities for system-wide collaborations, like QuestionPoint, to supplement core services. Our commitment to our users remains steadfast, and we are determined to adapt and fulfill our mission in the face of what will certainly be more years of budget challenges.

Bookend

WE WANT TO thank the librarians at UC Santa Cruz for courageously sharing their successes and failures in this case study.

In 1997, Neil Howe and William Strauss published *The Fourth Turning,* arguing that history can be seen as a series of four-stage cycles of recurring social or mood eras, which they call turnings. Each turning cycle works through roughly 80 years of boom (or High) through Awakening to Unraveling to Crisis. According to the Strauss-Howe theory, we're in the midst of a cyclical mood shift, turning from a period of Unraveling into a period of Crisis. Strauss and Howe suggest that the historical result of a crisis replaces old orders and dysfunctional institutions with a new order created from the seeds of the old. In order to prepare for the coming crisis, Strauss and Howe walk readers through a process that contains elements of a classic planned abandonment analysis, including focusing on core values, paying attention to new norms and data points, and looking for support from a variety of perspectives.[2] The purpose of the process is to ensure that individuals—and by extrapolation, organizations like libraries—are functional and diversified enough to withstand a Crisis and grow into the next societal High. While generational stereotypes and prophecies of the sort that Strauss and Howe deliver might be polarizing and a bit hyperbolic, in the end their theory leads us back to where we started—working to ensure that we can weather change with grace and compassion through proper planning and analysis.

If we're already following the advice of Drucker, Hesselbein, and our own common sense, we know we can't wait for an economic or medical crisis, or any sort of turning, to analyze library services. The time is always now.

REFERENCES

1. Fred Shapiro, "Quotes Uncovered: Who Said No Crisis Should Go to Waste?" *Freakonomics: The Hidden Side to Everything,* August 13, 2009, www.freakonomics.com/2009/08/13/quotes-uncovered-who-said-no-crisis-should-go-to-waste.

2. William Strauss and Neil Howe, *The Fourth Turning* (New York: Broadway, 1997), 316–320.

Case Study 6 | # University of North Carolina at Charlotte

PARTICIPANT OBSERVATION IS a key research method among cultural anthropologists. By closely observing how individuals in groups perform tasks or rituals over time, a detailed ethnographic understanding can be developed. Often this kind of observation can reveal differences in what participants say they do, or even believe they do, and what's really going on. It's one additional way to counteract magical thinking. Engineers and designers have used anthropological style research for years as a way to determine consumer needs and create innovative products. We can do the same things to improve libraries.

Anthropological studies of student services in libraries started with the University of Rochester's Undergraduate Research Project in 2004. The University of Rochester's groundbreaking study of student research habits gave librarians the tools and information to be truly student centered. Over the next several years, other libraries have started similar projects in an attempt to better know and better design services for their populations. As Lisa Nickel and Elizabeth Ladner illustrate in their case study of the academic library at the University of North Carolina at Charlotte, anthropological research can help to uncover some powerful planned abandonment ideas.

A New Way to Think

Anthropological Research Uncovers Powerful Ideas

Lisa T. Nickel and Elizabeth H. Ladner

The University of North Carolina (UNC) at Charlotte is North Carolina's urban research university, located in the state's largest metropolitan area with an enrollment of more than 25,000 students. UNC Charlotte is among the fastest growing universities in the 16-campus University of North Carolina System. The university maintains a particular commitment to addressing the cultural, economic, educational, environmental, health, and social needs of the greater Charlotte region.[1]

The J. Murrey Atkins Library at UNC Charlotte employs 33 librarians and 57 staff.

Letting Go of Legacy Services

The freedom to let go of legacy services and try new and innovative ideas is a rare occurrence in academic libraries. The J. Murrey Atkins Library at the University of North Carolina at Charlotte was presented with just such an opportunity when a new University Librarian was hired in August 2009. The timing was right for the library to recruit a "visionary" to provide dynamic leadership, as the university was entering a new five-year Strategic Planning cycle (2010–2015). One of the first projects undertaken under this new leadership was the development of a Brand Campaign for the library to communicate its focal message: "Atkins Library: A New Way to Think." This mindset laid the groundwork for the progressive changes of the next three years.

The examination of strategic direction provided the University Librarian with the opportunity to examine everything we were doing from a fresh perspective, assuring that the new goals being set for the library aligned with the new goals for the University. In addition, library staffing, resources, and services could be examined on a macro level to ensure that human and financial resources were being allocated in a way that not only maximized efficiency and effectiveness, but set the library on a path consistent with emerging academic library trends. To this end, the library hired consultants with expertise in academic library planning and organization to study the library's current operations and make recommendations consistent with our new goals.

Many of the consultants' recommendations have been implemented, and have resulted in major changes in the organizational structure of the library over a two-year period. While some of the greatest changes have occurred in Technical Services and Special Collections, Access Services has also been impacted. This case study will describe the decision making behind these changes and discuss the methods used in evaluating the services that we canceled and/or changed.

Methods and Data Used

We used a variety of methods and data to evaluate our services:

- qualitative data from the Library Ethnography Project
- statistical data
- anecdotal patron suggestions/comments
- staff expertise
- salary data to compute cost of services

Anthropologist in the Library

The new University Librarian, Stanley Wilder, came to UNC Charlotte from the University of Rochester, where he worked with a library anthropologist. One of the first major hiring decisions was to hire a library anthropologist to study how the students and faculty at UNC Charlotte do their work. The library anthropologist is a permanent member of the library faculty and contributes information gained from observations, interviews, photo diaries, and so forth, to library staff and faculty in order to inform our decision making with regard to services and policies.

Specific examples of how ethnographic research has resulted in improvements to library services include:

Redesign of the website and web development process, as described in Somaly Kim Wu, and Donna Lanclos (2001) "Re-imagining the users' experience: An ethnographic approach to web usability and space design," *Reference Services Review*, 39 no. 3, pp. 369–389):

> By turning to a research-based model of library policy, we have changed the
> way things look in our physical and digital spaces, and also how the library

works, how decisions are made, and the kinds of information that informs those decisions. Ethnography and usability, as driving forces in library policy, shift the impetus of decision making from top-down set priorities to priorities that diffuse upwards from patron needs, from patron work requirements.

Ethnographic practices can provide information that surveys and other self-reporting methods cannot. Methods that direct us to the perspective of our patrons, and allow us to be surprised by their thoughts and actions, ground us in their everyday practices and motives. Participant observation and open-ended interviews can be particularly effective in revealing the gap between what people say they do, and what they actually do. Used in combination with more traditional information gathering strategies (such as surveys, environmental scans, etc.), ethnographic techniques are powerful tools, and can be wielded to great effect in the crafting of library policy, including approaches to the configuration of our physical and digital spaces.

> The constant presence of ethnography, and of research-based decision processes, transforms the library as a whole into an experimental space.

In using ethnography to gain knowledge of patron needs and practices, we become a more agile library, one that responds more organically to the workflow of the university in which we are embedded. The constant presence of ethnography, and of research-based decision processes, transforms the library as a whole into an experimental space, one in which we try solutions that are based on one interpretation of the facts, and then continue to study behavior to evaluate whether or not we were correct. Because research is a constant in our process, we have the ability to recognize when we are on the right (or wrong) track, and recalibrate.[2]

Facilities use: Using information about the increasing amount of collaborative work that students at UNC Charlotte need to do made an argument for configuring spaces within the library that are appropriate for group work. This resulted in the reconfiguration of the library's ground floor in 2010 to be a collaborative group study area. Space pre-2010 was filled with study carrels and had no computers, which made for a quiet, solitary study area. Space post-spring 2010 was filled with whiteboards on the walls, sofas and armchairs, coffee tables and end tables (each with glass tops), and long tables (with embedded power outlets and glass partitions), which resulted in much more collaborative study and work. The furniture was arranged so that the long tables helped serve as partitions between group study areas (defined by the couches facing the whiteboards) as well as places for students to work either singly or in groups

Using information about how students used the new collaborative space provided an argument for expanding the possibilities available to students on the ground floor, in the form of additional study spaces around a new North Entrance. The new spaces include a glass-walled study room, also equipped with a screen for work-sharing, so that students can write on the glass walls like whiteboards, and share the work from their laptops to their fellow group-members. T1 touch tables allow a different kind of work-sharing never before possible in the library building (http://nineronline.com/2012/north-entrance-of-library-brings-new-student-workspace). The new North Entrance spaces also allow us to study what students are doing in these spaces, in groups and singly, so that we can plan for a further expansion of student spaces into the remainder of the ground floor.

Public services: knowledge of how students get information about the resources they need for their academic work was gathered not just from subject liaisons, but also from interview and photo diary data collected by the library ethnographer, as well as by her graduate and undergraduate researchers. Such data indicated that students primarily rely on peers and faculty members for their initial connection to resources, and that contact with subject liaisons is far more likely to happen in classroom contexts (either face to face, or on Moodle, the university's Learning Management System). To meet that reality, a Moodle block was developed to more effectively insert library resources into students' everyday classroom contexts. In addition, desk services were consolidated, and subject liaisons were moved off of the reference desk so that they could devote more time to working with students in their offices, in classrooms, and in labs.

Changes to Legacy Services

CAMPUS BOOK DELIVERY

In response to a rapidly growing campus, the library developed a new book delivery service called "Atkins Express." This began as a pilot project with minimal service (started with faculty from one or two departments for a summer) but quickly expanded to serve the entire faculty. Patrons use the "request" function in the library catalog to initiate the service: books are retrieved from the stacks and either held for students at the circulation desk or delivered to faculty offices via campus mail. We saw this as a branding opportunity, so we ordered permanent fabric zippered canvas mailing bags that clearly displayed the library's logo. The "Atkins Express" service, while starting as a physical delivery service using campus mail, has now expanded further with the purchase of an electric delivery van and several strategically located book drops across campus. Our Stacks Maintenance Manager has incorporated this pickup and delivery service into his work routine, so it required no additional staffing.

As a result of the positive feedback the library received, as well as evaluating the decline in Interlibrary Loan (ILL) scanning, the service has since expanded to include scanning and delivery of items from the library's own physical collection, within Fair Use guidelines. This work has been taken on by the Interlibrary Loan staff, who were able to assume this new responsibility with no additional staffing since ILL requests have declined in recent years.

Through the course of campus conversations and interviews, the library's anthropologist identified the book and article delivery service as a popular topic among graduate and doctoral students who wanted to have all of the same advantages in library service as faculty. We evaluated staff time and the level of requests and made the decision that we could include graduate students into this popular and growing service. Article delivery is now available to all graduate and doctoral students, while additional book delivery service is now offered to PhD students who have a physical office on campus. And, as described below, we use the same service to include campus delivery of physical ILL items to faculty and doctoral students.

LONGER CHECKOUTS

As a result of additional research completed by the library's anthropologist, we determined that faculty members and graduate students were not satisfied with the length of time they were allowed to keep library materials. This has become more of a concern because of at least two factors: the rapid expansion of the campus size over the past 10 years, and the rapidly increasing proportion of library resources available electronically—resulting in less frequent visits to the library by faculty/grad students. In addition, the library now provides desktop delivery of both Interlibrary Loan material as well as scanning and delivery of library-owned resources. As a result of all these factors, policies were changed to allow faculty, staff, graduate, and undergraduate students longer checkout periods, increasing from 120 days to 180 days, and increasing the number of renewals allowed, from two to three.

Once the decision was made in Access Services, library staff members were told of the change. There was little to no reaction internally. When the change was communicated to faculty, there was an immediate positive response: many of the positive comments came as a direct reply to the campus e-mail. This increase in the faculty loan period has resulted in much good will toward the library as well as increased use of the library collection. The number of books circulated to faculty and graduate students has actually increased by 128 percent for faculty since 2007 (see figure 6.1). We attribute this rise to longer borrowing periods, as well as the ease of campus book delivery. The only downside was an unintended consequence: as faculty/grad students are keeping items out for longer periods, there are now more items out at any given time. This resulted in the need to purchase more permanent canvas mailing bags to support this increased flow of materials between offices and the library.

FINES

Atkins Library had been collecting fines from students throughout its entire existence, despite the fact that the library itself did not benefit from the revenues. The library typically collected between $20,000 to $25,000 per year in fines that were returned to the State of North Carolina. The process of collecting these fines was very time-intensive for staff, required cumbersome processes, and generated inevitable disputes with patrons. It was estimated that collection of fines cost the library $8,645 per year in staff time alone—and, as stated above, the library saw no direct benefit from this service.

Philosophically, the collection of fines does not serve the library's mission, and there is frequently negative reaction from patrons who have to pay these fines. The University Librarian consulted with the Provost, who agreed that whether or not to collect fines was a library decision. Consequently, the most burdensome and least productive category of fines was eliminated: student fines for General Collections material. Fines are still collected for Laptops, Reserves, and Interlibrary Loan items.

Additional policy changes have resulted in a flat $100 fee for lost items, rather than custom pricing and billing for each lost book. Operations are now streamlined by the elimination of the most time-consuming and least productive portion of collecting and billing, and staff members consequently have more time to spend on reserves processing and special projects.

As a result of these policy changes, students were thrilled with the elimination of fines, as were librarians, library staff, and the University Librarian, who was able to announce this elimination of fines as a positive new change at a time when students were dealing with increased tuition and larger classes. The positive reaction was instantaneous. Students frequently thanked staff members working at the desks. One faculty member questioned the decision, citing "teaching students to be responsible" as a possible reason to continue fines, but Access Services staff members were happy with this decision. We can't design our policies to teach students responsibility.

INTERLIBRARY LOAN

Soon after the changes in circulation policies took place, staffing and patterns of use in the Interlibrary Loan (ILL) department were evaluated. Several factors were in play. New leadership in the library was successful in obtaining money to increase our electronic collections of books and journals. Staff members in ILL also noticed a greater availability of free full-text articles by journals on the open web. As a result, our patrons' requests for electronic items through ILL dropped 15 percent. However, requests for physical items increased by 29 percent. We attribute this increase to enhanced discoverability provided by a well-functioning discovery tool purchased from EBSCO, called EBSCO Discovery Service. This created a noticeable change in the workload of ILL staff. Staff had more downtime and the bulk of the work shifted to the Lending side. Requests from other libraries for our books increased. So, in an effort to compensate, we moved Borrowing personnel to Lending and reduced one borrowing position to half-time, which saved approximately $15,000.

Additional savings have come from streamlining services in the ILL process where the staff has implemented the "trusted lenders" program, resulting in approximately 90 percent of our patrons' electronic items being delivered directly from the lender to the patron with no intervention on our part.

In addition to evaluating staffing patterns in ILL, we looked at all positions and support involved in ILL. We evaluated the time, effort, and skills needed in order to maintain and upgrade our own ILLiad server. One staff member in the library's Information Technology Systems department had responsibility for scheduling, troubleshooting, and upgrading our ILLiad software. Factors such as reasonable cost and easy availability of knowledgeable offsite technicians helped make our decision to move to a hosted solution. Abandoning our own ILLiad-hosted solution has been a seamless transition and resulted in virtually no negative service impact.

Following these functional changes, we have also discontinued using ARIEL in ILL since it has been a somewhat problematic (and less frequently used) software system with no added value for us. In our experience, smaller schools and libraries in Canada, New Zealand, and Australia make up the majority of ARIEL users and are not a large percentage of our use. We can instead use ARIEL's e-mail option to receive items from these locations. In addition, we are a member of the Association of Southeastern Research Libraries (ASERL) and participate in their Kudzu rapid ILL program, which provides expedited delivery of materials from member libraries.

As a result of these changes, and patterns of patron requests, our ILL staff has more time available to process electronic delivery of items from the library's own collection for our faculty and graduate students. Additionally, staff members have a great deal of downtime in the summer, enabling them to work on projects that can benefit other areas in the library.

Less Popular Changes

EQUIPMENT

One of the library's most popular services had been the purchase and circulation of equipment of many types to support academic endeavors. Sample equipment included:

- digital cameras
- digital camcorders
- digital voice recorders
- microphones
- scientific calculators
- public address megaphone
- large speakers
- cassette players/recorders
- televisions with VCRs or DVD players
- film screens

Despite the popularity of this service, the new leadership in the library decided that this service did not fit within the library's strategic mission, and the decision was made to eliminate the equipment purchase/circulation service—with the critical exception of laptops. As indicated in the Gate Count Statistics (see figure 6.1) patron visits (overwhelmingly students) increased by 47 percent over the past three years, and much of this demand for the library's spaces has been for access to computers (both desktop and circulating laptops)—so laptop circulation has continued to be supported as part of the library's and the university's mission to support student academics.

The decision to eliminate equipment circulation as a library service was hastened when the funding for upgrades/repairs was denied by the university. The University Librarian decided to spend available money on something that could benefit more students: laptops. The Head of Access Services communicated the decision to library staff, including the library communications officer who assisted in creating an e-mail that was sent to the entire campus. Since certain faculty members depended on the library to provide equipment for their students and built entire assignments around the available equipment, the announcement was planned in order to provide faculty with time to adjust their syllabi and make adjustments to curricula. Despite these measures, the reaction across campus was not positive. Much discussion followed and as a result, the library was able to transfer some equipment to various departments who would manage this equipment internally. The entire process shed light on:

- the need for the library to clearly communicate its primary mission: supporting student learning and research;
- the importance of clear, firm communication to all stakeholders: library faculty and staff as well as students, faculty and staff across campus; and
- the importance of planning.

This decision was painful for a few months, but the ensuing conversations about costs and staffing helped educate campus stakeholders about issues faced by the library in times of economic stress. The campus has now adjusted to this new service model, and they no longer look to the library for this type of equipment support.

Justification for this decision bears explanation. Circulation statistics for the equipment were high (see figure 6.1) and would have suggested that we not stop this service. However, as part of the strategic planning and evaluation process, library administration required all staff to focus on the core services of the library. One full position was devoted to the following functions related to the equipment: purchasing, maintaining, instructing in the use of, replacing, repairing, inventorying, and issuing fines. Upon discontinuing equipment circulation that position was redirected to assist with the library's new expanded book and article delivery service, "Atkins Express." Positive outcomes from abandoning the equipment service have been an increased focus on the very popular laptop lending program and additional support for busy services by the staff member who was formerly dedicated to the equipment program. This

FIG. 6.1 **Evaluating Changes in Service**

ACCESS SERVICES	2007/08	2010/11	% Change
CIRCULATION			
Books, avs, documents, periodicals circulated	92,429	90,818	-2%
Equipment circulated	22,283	6,878	-69%
Laptops circulated	15,876	31,733	100%
Number of physical reserve items circulated	14,852	6,487	-56%
Total Circulation	**145,440**	**135,916**	-7%
Students	21,354	28,030	31%
Faculty	1,604	3,653	128%
Staff	1,371	1,769	29%
Community	981	2,357	140%
RESERVES			
Number of items on reserve (print and electronic)	7,740	11,681	51%
Number of class lists accessed	51,393	49,502	-4%
Number of individual documents accessed	70,343	75,995	8%
Number of new faculty accounts established	143	656	359%
INTERLIBRARY LOAN			
Lending (from Atkins Library to other libraries)			
Electronic items	3,158	2,615	-17%
Physical items	5,546	6,486	17%
Borrowing (from other libraries to Atkins)			
Electronic items	8,546	7,225	-15%
Physical items	4,056	5,233	29%
Stacks maintenance			
Number of items reshelved	172,311	155,751	-10%
Gate count			
Number of patrons using library facility	906,578	1,330,250	47%
Atkins Express Services (2008/09–2010/11 data)			
Number of books retrieved	3,489	3,520	1%
Number of books delivered	2,354	2,603	11%
Total number of requests	5,843	6,123	5%
Number of articles delivered	2,099	1,514	-28%
Articles provided to dist ed students	216	100	-54%
ARCHITECTURE LIBRARY			
Circulation	5,229	4,262	-18%
Equipment circulated	770	1,750	127%
Reserves times accessed	62	50	-19%
Gate Count	66,195	64,300	-3%

person now retrieves items on hold, packages and mails items to faculty, and processes returns of those same materials. She also has enough time to assist as needed in Interlibrary Loan and Course Reserves.

In retrospect, the decision to stop equipment lending should have been communicated to campus much further in advance. A full semester's notice might have been adequate timing, or it may have just provided a longer period for faculty to fully understand the implications for their assignments. The library should have created a better system to surplus the outdated equipment to campus departments. These lessons will be remembered in future decisions of this magnitude.

Positive Outcomes of Abandoning Legacy Services

COLLABORATION WITH OTHER LIBRARY UNITS

As in most academic libraries, demand for services such as Interlibrary Loan and Reserves drops sharply during the summer months. Acknowledging the increasing emphasis being put on digitization efforts, particularly within the Special Collections Unit, the Head of Access Services offered to have ILL and Reserves staff volunteers trained to provide robust Dublin Core metadata description for digital images, including photographs to be included in the library's digital collections. This not only kept Access Services staff productive year-round, but it has also given the staff who participated a new skill set. The outcome is that a collection of photographs previously inaccessible is now available to historians and scholars throughout the world, and staff members have developed new and marketable skills.

LIBRARY ANTHROPOLOGIST

Working with an anthropologist in our library has resulted in creating a culture of continual research and assessment. Library staff and faculty have begun to rely on non-traditional methods to solicit feedback, like placing rolling whiteboards with questions on them in various areas of the library. Students have become more willing to tell us how they feel about changes in the library—using the whiteboards, social media avenues, and, more regularly, in person. Staff and library faculty have also become accustomed to continually evaluating their workflow and everyday processes in order to anticipate changes in demand and look for ways to increase service to students and efficiencies in the process.

Conclusion

All of these decisions to abandon legacy services were part of a drive to have the library focus on our core mission: "The J. Murrey Atkins Library at the University of North Carolina Charlotte advances intellectual discovery by connecting people with knowledge." Under this new paradigm of continual assessment and responsive change, library staff and faculty feel free to examine and revise outdated procedures, or analyze declining statistics, where in the past they feared losing positions. Our successful redeployment of staff to work on projects outside of their home department has reinforced the philosophy that everyone should work together for the greater good of the library and the university.

Bookend

AS WE SEE from the UNC Charlotte case study, the freedom to try new things can sometimes go awry. Their process to stop circulating equipment met with resistance from the campus, but they persisted, knowing that in an era of negative budget growth, they could not innovate in meaningful ways while still maintaining all of their past practices. Bill Cosby, educator and comedian, famously admitted that "I don't know the key to success, but the key to failure is trying to please everybody." But as many cognitive scientists are revealing, failure and uncertainty aren't bad—in fact, in science failure is something to be cultivated. We often learn just as much, or sometimes even more from things that don't go as planned. But what happens when we can't even plan?

In the article "Newspapers and Thinking the Unthinkable," Clay Shirky argues that newspapers weren't surprised by the advent of the Internet, indeed, they saw it "from miles off" and came up with multiple plans for dealing with its potential to disrupt the marketplace. However, newspapers failed to think the "unthinkable" and realize that they were living in a true revolution that would completely destroy their business model. "Society doesn't need newspapers. What we need is journalism," Shirky claims. Shirky lays out the issues, but does not pretend to have an answer for saving newspapers or journalism. Noting that newspapers are broken, Shirky states "That is what real revolutions are like. The old stuff gets broken faster than the new stuff is put in its place." Everything and nothing might be the next step in solving the newspaper dilemma.[3]

David W. Lewis, Dean of the IUPUI University Library and Indiana University Assistant Vice President for Digital Scholarly Communications, takes Shirky's essay and applies it to libraries in an article from *Indiana Libraries*. Lewis argues that contemporary newspapers and libraries have grown out of the same 19th century model resulting from the industrialization of printing. Dewey and others developed the modern library to "manage large numbers of relatively scarce documents."[4] Lewis explores how the same forces revolutionizing the newspaper industry are also disrupting how libraries obtain, organize, store, and disseminate content. We are living and working in a brave new digitized world, and no one knows what to make of it. Shirky and Lewis both argue that the only valid response is to try new things, "even if they seem crazy and fail."[5] If things we try don't work out, that's okay, that's part of the process. Let it go. We will always be trying out things and some ideas will stick, some will fail and some will lead to even better solutions. What we need are librarians with the ability and grace to try and fail and move ever forward.

Sometimes failure is a clear sign that the failed service should be abandoned. But it's not always so simple. In the midst of a disruptive innovation, it can be difficult for even the most radical thinkers to make clear-eyed choices. These difficult choices are why we need to return to our core values as librarians, and make data-driven decisions based on research and framed within our values. We might not all be able to emulate the kinds of research performed by UNC Charlotte's resident library anthropologist, but we can all identify tools and resources at hand to make our decisions a little bit easier.

REFERENCES

1. University of North Carolina, "About UNC Charlotte," accessed July 18, 2011, www.uncc.edu/landing/about.

2. Somaly Kim Wu and Donna Lanclos, "Re-imagining the Users' Experience: An Ethnographic Approach to Web Usability and Space Design," *Reference Services Review* 39, no. 3 (2011): 369–389.

3. Clay Shirky, "Newspapers and Thinking the Unthinkable," www.shirky.com/weblog/2009/03/newspapers-and-thinking-the-unthinkable.

4. David W. Lewis, "A Strategy for Academic Libraries in the First Quarter of the 21st Century," *College & Research Libraries* 68, no. 5 (2007): 54

5. Ibid., 57.

Case Study 7 | **American University**

PEOPLE ARE THE key element in any change; even the most data-driven decision-making process requires people to support and implement the change. In Anne Elguindi's case study featuring American University, we see an example of how data compelled all aspects of the decision to make change in acquiring and processing electronic resources. In the University of Arizona's case study, we saw the importance of process. In this instance, we see how vital it is to get people involved in all aspects of the process, and can start to develop models of data-driven decision making for our own organizations.

During a 2012 presentation to the joint Maryland/Delaware Library Association, we discovered that staff buy-in to decisions was a key element vexing many library administrators. One director termed it "the murmuring." The phrase caught on and sparked discussion throughout our three-hour session. How do we control the murmuring? How can we turn the interest and dedication behind the murmurs into a force for positive change? Elguindi shows one possible method, by dealing directly with the "murmuring" through programmatic strategic planning with a wide cross section of staff, and setting up her division for success.

A Focus on Buy-in

Facilitating the Shift to Electronic Resources through Collaborative
Strategic Planning

Anne C. Elguindi

ALTHOUGH MANY LIBRARIES spend the majority of their materials budgets on electronic resources, they often only have a small percentage of their personnel dedicated to supporting these resources. Believing that there needed to be a general shift to more staffing attention for the electronic environment, but recognizing that the path forward through such significant change can be difficult, I held a series of planning sessions for the Information Delivery Services (IDS) division at American University Library, a division that combines the traditional library functions of technical services and access services. The goal was to gather ideas from the many excellent minds in the division in charting our path forward but also to get buy-in from the people who would be directly affected.

The approach detailed below has much in common with what other libraries are actively engaged in. It is similar in theme to what Sarah M. Pritchard described for Northwestern University, which included the need to rethink the library's services, collections, and physical space in the context of the digital environment while recognizing that the library's basic goals and values have not changed.[1]

It is similar in approach to the work done in strategic planning at the University of Arizona, as it builds from general areas of change; in "From Surviving to Thriving," Cheryl J. Stoffle and Cheryl Cuillier went into depth about five categories of thinking about the future of libraries: Organizational Structure and Culture; Planning and Budgeting; Communication; Collections, Discoverability, Access, and Delivery; and Library as Service.[2] It is similar in structure to what many libraries (and other organizations) use in their strategic planning processes, building from larger scoped concepts to specific actions. Richard Wayne, as just one example, outlined the general process for strategic planning at the University of Texas Southwestern Medical Center at Dallas Library, from the creation of a vision statement to forming themes, two-year goals, and objectives.[3]

Library literature about strategic planning, however, often remains at the theme or goal level and attempts to deal with library-wide issues. What makes this discussion of strategic planning different is that it focuses on the point of development from strategic goal to specific action for particular areas of the library: access and technical services. Included are the motivation and rationale for developing the strategic planning process, the specific procedures used, the results, and plans for the future.

Defining Information Delivery Services

The IDS division is made up of four principle areas: Access Services, Acquisitions, Cataloging Services, and Electronic Resources Management. Access Services is further divided into four areas: Circulation and Stacks, Interlibrary Loan, Reserves, and Technology Services. This division was created in a 2008 library-wide reorganization after an evaluation by R2 Consulting. Previously, Access Services had been administratively linked to other public services such as Reference and Media Services. The other IDS units (with Electronic Resource Management defined as Serials at the time) had been together within Collection Services.

In many ways, the combination of services and functions within IDS makes sense. It has brought together the units that represent the full post-selection workflow of materials, including licensing, purchasing, resource description, resource management, and patron access. It has also decreased the distance between technical services and the library's patrons, since the topics discussed within the division are more user-based than discussions typically held within technical services.

This combination of services and functions, however, also put units in close administrative proximity that have significant cultural differences. The technical services have had a long history of flexible scheduling, where unit members can work less than five days per week by working more hours per day or can adjust their working hours to either earlier or later than the general 9 to 5 schedule. In Access Services, due to the staffing needs of service desks, full-time staff members often have nights and weekends in their regular schedules, and flexible schedules, because they would require participation from all of those in a given unit.

There are also general differences in responsibilities across the two broadly defined units of technical and access services. In Access Services, all full-time staff members must function as managers to some degree because the unit is highly dependent on student workers to complete much of the work, both in processing materials and in staffing service desks. In Technical Services, however, many full-time staff work independently, and full-time staffing is used to do the vast majority of the work.

These are not negatives, because the diversity of roles and responsibilities within the division also means that there is a broader range of viewpoints. It does mean, however, that strategic planning within the IDS division must give careful attention to ensuring that all viewpoints are heard, and building consensus through conversation is critical.

IDS Planning As Part of a Larger Whole

The university and the library engage in a structured and programmatic strategic planning process. The university administration develops goals, the library develops goals from the university goals, and the library-wide goals cascade down through the divisions and units, eventually playing a role in forming the annual work plans for all full-time staff members. The 2011–2012 objectives for the Information Delivery Services division, for example, are as follows:

- In collaboration with the collection managers, continue to provide materials in desired formats and shift from print to electronic where appropriate
- Enable more intuitive, improved access to library materials in all formats
- Contribute to improving physical space within the library
- Ensure that library staff members are getting the training that they need, both from outside sources and cross-training within the library, in order to enhance skills and promote growth
- Effectively share information across the units and across the library
- Provide service that meets user needs efficiently and effectively

The library has also developed a mission statement:

The University Library enables educational and research success by:
- building collections and facilitating access to information across all formats;
- teaching people how to locate, assess, and use information to meet their needs;
- providing welcoming spaces that support a full range of intellectual endeavors.

And there is an official shortened version: "We enable success."

In addition, the library has used the LibQUAL+ survey every two years since 2001 to get feedback from the campus community. These survey results are shared throughout the library. Many staff members across the IDS division were on the project team for LibQUAL+ in the past cycle, and they gave a presentation to the full division about the 2011 results with a focus on areas of interest to the division.

An increased focus on the shift to the electronic environment was therefore not out of the blue but a natural outgrowth of previous high-level planning and assessment in the university, library, and division. The need was to turn the goals for the year, many of which relate to the shift to the electronic environment, into specific actions. The concept of going digital was widely understood, but the division had not taken the time as a whole to step back and discuss what this really meant for services and staffing.

Outlining the Planning Process

Although it was clear that IDS needed to engage in planning and discussion to move the division forward in a proactive way, it was not clear how best to start that process. The IDS division is large, with 32 full-time staff members and 60 part-time staff members, most of whom are student workers, and the hours of coverage for the service desks are long, requiring divergent schedules. This makes it difficult to get everyone together for meetings, and all-division meetings of the full-time staff take place only every two months. Due to the large number of people in what is often a small room, divisional meetings are most often used for updates about issues that affect the library as a whole or for presentations by IDS staff members about their new initiatives or what they learned by attending a recent training session or conference.

Given that the full divisional meetings were a difficult fit with strategic planning, I approached this project with a number of requirements in mind:

- The overall strategic planning process of the university and library had been fairly top-down, and although I wanted this new planning to be in line with that work, I also wanted a fairly fresh start of listening to what people in the division had to say.
- We needed extended time together, not a series of one-hour meetings, for a thoughtful process.
- I wanted to incorporate in-person and asynchronous discussion to accommodate different preferences for communication.

- Due to the cultural differences and different perspectives across the division, I wanted to ensure that conversation took place across the areas of the division.
- I wanted to incorporate prioritizing possible actions into the process but in an efficient way.
- As the four unit heads (Head of Access Services, Acquisitions Librarian, Metadata Librarian, and Electronic Resources Management Librarian) have a weekly meeting together with me as the IDS Administrative Team where we discuss planning issues, I wanted to focus on feedback from staff members who were not unit heads.

Out of these requirements came the following approach, which is discussed in more detail in the sections that follow:

- An extended meeting of the high-level staff and faculty within the division (14 of the 32 full-time personnel).
- An online review and discussion of the results from that meeting.
- A prioritization of actions by the full division with the opportunity to contribute new actions through a second meeting, this time of all the full-time personnel.
- An approval of the plan for moving forward by the IDS Administrative Team.

The First IDS Strategic Planning Forum

The first planning session was a three-hour forum held in October 2011 with all the high-level staff and faculty in the division. Staff members at the university are organized into bands, and IDS has three of these bands: Specialist, Coordinator, and Project Leader. The higher staff members are in the band structure, the more their jobs are usually associated with strategic planning, so I included faculty (the librarians in the division, although many staff members also have a Master's Degree in Library Science), Project Leaders, and Coordinators.

This was one of the most difficult decisions of organizing this planning process. I was reluctant to exclude any full-time personnel from this initial forum, but I did feel that I needed a small enough group to have some group discussion as part of the session, and to have all the full-time IDS staff engaged in a session for three hours would have been difficult given the needs of the library. Using the staff band structure at least gave me a defensible rationale, and the number of participants, fourteen, felt like a manageable size.

At the beginning of the forum, I gave a few introductory comments about all ideas being welcome and everyone in libraries today needing to be comfortable with change. I also highlighted how electronic resources have grown to be the majority of the library's collections but that the division staff's responsibilities had not necessarily made that change along with the collection. I then presented the structure for the forum. The forum was organized around a series of small group conversations based on four major areas: Collections, Services, Workflow and Infrastructure, and Defining the Library. In an effort to generate conversation, I handed out Taiga Forum Provocative Statements (www.taiga-forum.org) that I had organized according to these four areas. The Taiga Forum is a gathering of Assistant/Associate University Librarians/Deans/Directors that comes together to discuss areas of potential change and transformation in libraries. In 2006, 2009, and 2011, the members of the Taiga Forum drafted and distributed Provocative Statements that were intended to spark conversation within academic libraries.

In order to ensure that everyone talked with people from other areas of the division and with different people throughout the forum, I had prepared a list of people for each group for each of the four conversations, ensuring that each group had members from different units within the division and that individuals rarely had two groups in common. I and three of the unit heads were notetakers for the conversations so that we would be more in the role of listeners than speakers, although all were invited to contribute to the conversations.

All the groups were charged with discussing the areas of change and suggesting possible actions we could take as a division to better respond to current trends and what we saw as the future of our library. Each group was given 25 minutes to discuss the topic at hand before rotating to a new group and new topic. At the end of the small group discussions, we gathered together as a whole to report back about what each small group had come up with. We went through each of the four areas and asked the notetakers to report to the full group about what their groups had talked about. This stimulated some further discussion and clarification.

Online Discussion

I had taken notes during the reporting session, and, after the meeting, I condensed the feedback from the session into a single document. Each main area had developed smaller themes that had emerged during the forum:

- **Collections:** E-Readers, The Increasing Importance of the Website, Shifts in Collection Development, The Changing Nature of the Book

- **Services:** Changes in Technology, Assessment, Services for Electronic Resources
- **Workflow and Infrastructure:** The Growth of Electronic Resources, Library Systems, Cross-Division Interaction, Shifts in Resource Description
- **Defining the Library:** The Electronic Environment, Online Learning, The Library Building

In the document, each new theme included a summarizing statement from the forum as well as suggested actions. Many of these showed how e-resources require a new blending across the public and technical services lines. Two examples follow:

Services for E-Resources: The majority of the materials budget goes toward electronic materials, but the majority of the public services staffing within IDS supports the print collection. There is room for growth of patron services for the electronic collection.

- Action: Share e-resource troubleshooting tickets to spread knowledge of the types of problems that users have more widely.
- Action: Consider new models of e-resource services that cover more hours of support and in-person help.

The Growth of Electronic Resources: Electronic resources require different workflows, systems, and skills. The library needs to ensure that its staffing fits its collections. What should the library infrastructure look like when we are 95 percent electronic and 5 percent print?

- Action: Extend the Electronic Resource Management System across the division, using project-based training like the book weeding project.
- Action: The organizational model we have is still fairly traditional and focused on the print collection. Consider alternate models that are a better fit for our division's changing collections and workflows.

This document was then put online in a Google document, and I invited all those who had been in the forum to comment on it. Comments people made to the document included sharing articles of interest, suggestions for additional actions, edits to wording, discussions about whether particular actions were necessary or possible, elaborations on the perceived needs of patrons, possible areas of partnership or conflict with other divisions, and specific training that would be needed to make actions possible.

The Second IDS Strategic Planning Forum

Based on the online conversation, I finalized the wording of the actions, and these actions were then taken to the full division in November 2011. As we discussed the actions in a group meeting, inviting those present to add actions for the group's consideration, I used a classroom clicker set to gather feedback.

Although clicker sets, or student response systems, are most often used in instructional sessions for students, many libraries have also found them to be useful in staff training sessions and meetings. Kim Granath and Sue Samson described the use of clickers in continuing education for reference staff at the University of Montana as part of a gaming approach;[4] Christina Hoffman and Susan Goodwin described the use of clickers in a library faculty and staff training session at Texas A&M University in order to make the session more interactive and encourage discussion, among other goals;[5] and Bobbie L. Collins, Rosalind Tedford, and H. David Womack described the use of clickers in library staff meetings at Wake Forest University to obtain feedback about strategic planning initiatives.[6] As clickers provide both active learning opportunities and response anonymity, they are particularly well suited to sessions in which the goal is to get a high level of participation and in which all voices are to be heard equally.

As goal setting often involves two factors—how important something is to do, or priority, as well as how easy it is to do, or feasibility—feedback using the clickers was structured so that everyone could rate the actions in these two areas. Priority was determined on a five-point scale from absolutely essential to not needed, and feasibility was determined on a three-point scale from easy to do to hard to do. Sample slides with responses from the forum are shown below (see figures 7.1–7.4).

As can be seen in the figures, these two factors in combination showed interesting trends among the staff members' answers. Promoting data management skills among library staff was viewed to be very important, for example, with almost all participants highlighting it as either absolutely essential or something the library should do, but half the participants also thought it might prove to be somewhat difficult to achieve. Other questions, such as evaluating the staffing models of other technology-related services across campus, showed more mixed results. Here, although there was a bump at "should do" for priority, significant numbers of staff also believed this to be absolutely essential, nice to do, or low priority. How easy this action would be to accomplish also showed distinct variety.

Although it did not represent the variety of opinions, an average did seem to be a fair mark of the group's overall opinion. Using the averages of the

FIG. 7.1

Make an effort to learn about mobile devices patrons are using to view library resources.

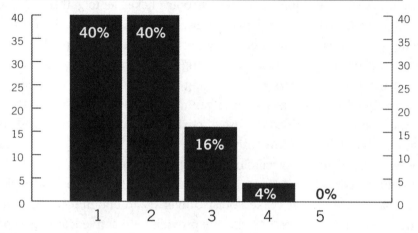

1: Absolutely Essential | 2: Should Do | 3: Would Be Nice | 4: Low Priority | 5: Not Needed

Make an effort to learn about mobile devices patrons are using to view library resources.

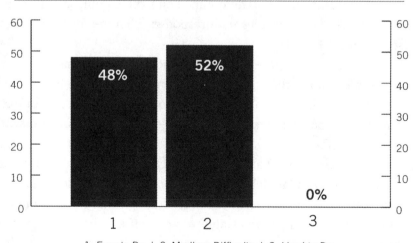

1: Easy to Do | 2: Medium Difficulty | 3: Hard to Do

FIG. 7.2

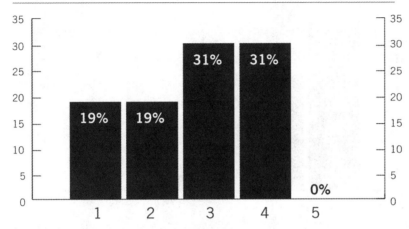

Investigate possibility of creating a more portal-like experience for library users

1: Absolutely Essential | 2: Should Do | 3: Would Be Nice | 4: Low Priority | 5: Not Needed

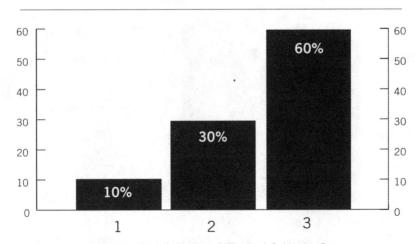

Investigate possibility of creating a more portal-like experience for library users

1: Easy to Do | 2: Medium Difficulty | 3: Hard to Do

FIG. 7.3

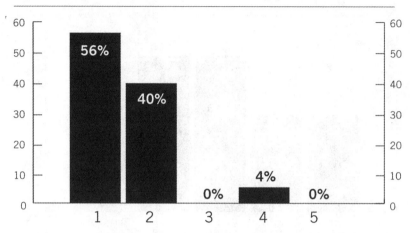

Promote and provide training for data management skills for library staff

1: Absolutely Essential | 2: Should Do | 3: Would Be Nice | 4: Low Priority | 5: Not Needed

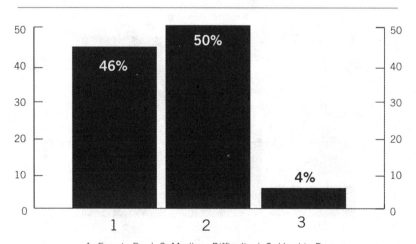

Promote and provide training for data management skills for library staff

1: Easy to Do | 2: Medium Difficulty | 3: Hard to Do

FIG. 7.4

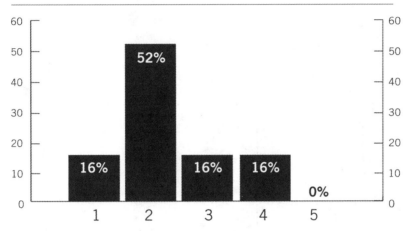

Evaluate the staffing models of other technology-related services across campus

1: Absolutely Essential | 2: Should Do | 3: Would Be Nice | 4: Low Priority | 5: Not Needed

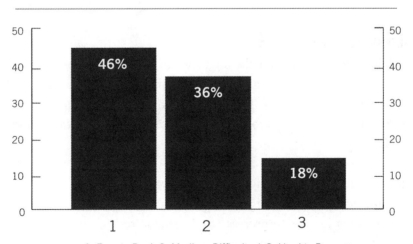

Evaluate the staffing models of other technology-related services across campus

1: Easy to Do | 2: Medium Difficulty | 3: Hard to Do

99

results for priority and feasibility from this session, I was able to chart out the actions according to these criteria. The actions were well distributed across the four quadrants, from high priority and relatively easy to accomplish to low priority and difficult to do, allowing for the development of a clear line for moving forward (see figure 7.5).

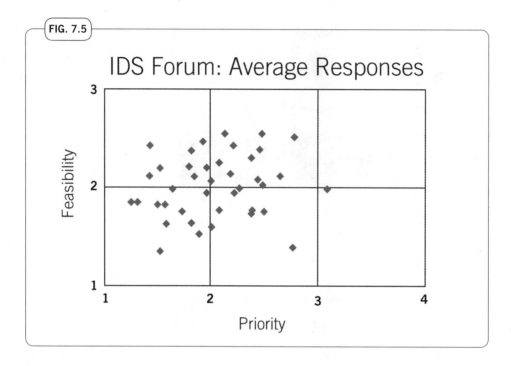

FIG. 7.5

IDS Forum: Average Responses

Finalized Actions

I wanted to focus initially on the high-priority items that people believed would be relatively easy to accomplish. I took these items to the IDS Administrative Team for consideration. The Team added a few items that were already in progress and a few easily accomplished items that might as well be included in the first stage.

The Team then divided the actions into new and continuing actions and outlined specific tasks for spring 2012. Many of these tasks were iterative steps toward achieving the larger actions in the plan. One of the finalized actions, for example, was to promote and provide training for data management skills for library staff, and a specific task for spring 2012 was to train the Digital Collections Cataloging Specialist to activate resources in the Electronic Resource Management System. Another action was to increase partnership with Collection Development to continuously assess usage of the collection and to get feedback from users about the collection. Specific tasks for this action were to standardize how Collection Managers ask for reports, such as through a web form, and build a file of reports.

Some of the actions involved what the division could stop doing in order to take on the new responsibilities. One of the finalized actions, for example, was to continue to advocate for the ability for the library to have one person dedicated fully to the website and its associated tools or at least a means to give those involved with the website more time for these responsibilities. The Technology Services Coordinator's position description had recently been rewritten to include substantial website editing, but due to other responsibilities, she had not been able to dedicate sufficient time to this project. This opened up conversations about what the division could give up in order to make this important responsibility possible, such as decreasing mediated copy services for patrons.

Other tasks were related to gathering data. The Head of Access Services, for example, was assigned the task of identifying institutions that excel at online learning and evaluating their library services with the eventual goal being to identify ways the division could improve its services to distance education and online learning students. For the action of acknowledging that more reference work is going through Access Services and responding with either more training or a request for more direct reference support, the task for spring 2012 was to run reports on the number of reference questions asked by patrons at the Access Services desks and compare these numbers to the number of informational questions asked at the reference desk.

This process also put current projects into a more structured planning tool. One of the finalized actions was to continue development of improved workflows and infrastructure for e-books, and the plan acknowledged that the division was already doing this through the implementation of the University of Notre Dame's CORAL Electronic Resource Management System (ERMS) as a workflow tool. As another example, a finalized action was to was implement cross-IDS training opportunities, and it was acknowledged that the recent pilot of having one of the Acquisitions Searchers work 20 percent of his time in the Interlibrary Loan Unit was a good test case for this. Identifying these projects in the context of a plan placed them in the larger picture and set the stage for assessing the results and basing future plans on the results of this assessment.

Conclusion and Future Plans

It has been incredibly difficult for libraries to keep pace with the rapid change to the electronic environment, largely because the work associated with physical format materials has not gone away. But it seems that all people who work in technical and access services will eventually need to be versed in the systems, skills, and concepts of electronic resource management if we are going to create truly effective services and collections for our users. The planning process outlined here did provide at least a basic infrastructure for enabling this change. As a division, we now have concrete ways to move forward, and we have the foundation of consensus and wide input to support those actions.

One of the key benefits of this process was including many full-time staff members. I received positive feedback from participants in the forums, and many took the time to tell me they appreciated being included. Although I did limit the attendees of the initial forum for what seemed like good reasons, in the future I would like to include all full-time staff and possibly student workers. This might be the most possible during the summer when service desk hours are shorter. This process also helped create awareness across the division of projects people were not completely aware of, particularly those that were only in development. Having themed discussions among people from many different units and coming together to discuss possible ways forward broadened the cross-unit knowledge within the division.

As we move forward, it will be a challenge to maintain awareness of the plan created and programmatically move through the areas because daily responsibilities can be all-consuming, but I believe this process has helped set the division up for success. If nothing else, this process allowed me to hear more from people within the division. Every day I feel lucky to work with such engaged, creative, and thoughtful people, and to take the time to hear their ideas for new services, challenges that patrons and library staff face, and predictions for the future was extremely valuable.

Bookend

ONE OF THE most remarkable things about the American University case study is the way that Elguindi used a variety of communication strategies to ensure success. Elguindi controlled the "murmuring" by including staff throughout a transparent change process. Elguindi emphasizes the importance of clearly communicating to staff, peers, and directors about ongoing service analyses, but it is also essential, once you have reached an internal decision to abandon a public service, to communicate with all of your users. Having, and following, a communications strategy is key to making lasting change stick.

There are two accepted precepts in marketing that should be applied when abandoning a service. The first is just when you are getting sick of what you're communicating, the audience is finally getting the message. So what may be old news to you and your staff still needs to be communicated to everyone else, and librarians and staff should use every possible vehicle available to announce the change in service. Remember that even though you may have been examining this service for months, your audience may be hearing it for the first time. The second marketing precept is that people need to hear something seven times before the message is retained. It is relatively simple to make sure that your news is repeated through the variety of communications channels available in your organization.

If we want things to be different in our libraries, we have to first change ourselves, and the way we respond to, plan for, and communicate change. It's a hard, but essential piece of the puzzle. Elguindi's method is not easy, and it takes time, but it works.

REFERENCES

1. Sarah M. Pritchard, "Deconstructing the Library: Reconceptualizing Collections, Spaces and Services," *Journal of Library Administration* 48, no. 2 (2008): 219–233.

2. Carla J. Stoffle and Cheryl Cuillier, "From Surviving to Thriving," *Journal of Library Administration* 51, no. 1 (2011): 130–155.

3. Richard Wayne, "The Academic Library Strategic Planning Puzzle: Putting the Pieces Together," *College & Research Libraries News* 72, no. 1 (January 2011): 12–15.

4. Kim Granath and Sue Samson, "Audience Response Systems: Beyond the Classroom," American Library Association Annual Conference Virtual Posters (2009), accessed January 28, 2014, http://presentations.ala.org/index.php?title =Audience_Response_Systems:_Beyond_the_Classroom.

5. Christina Hoffman and Susan Goodwin, "A Clicker for Your Thoughts: Technology for Active Learning," *New Library World* 107, no. 9/10 (2006): 422–433.

6. Bobbie L. Collins, Rosalind Tedford, and H. David Womack, "'Debating' the Merits of Clickers in an Academic Library," *North Carolina Libraries* (Spring/Summer 2008): 20–24.

Communication Strategies
for Successful Change

An Interview with Valerie Diggs

Mary Evangeliste

VALERIE DIGGS IS the K–12 Department Head of Libraries for the District of Chelmsford (Massachusetts). She serves as the high school librarian for Chelmsford High School, with a student population of 1,740. Valerie is a former classroom teacher, and holds a Master's Degree in Library Science and her certification as a School Library Media Specialist from Simmons College. She is also a doctoral candidate at the University of Massachusetts in Lowell in the Leadership in Schooling Program and serves as an adjunct professor at Simmons College in Boston, teaching Organization and Management of School Library Media Centers.

Valerie's interest in new learning spaces has revolutionized library services in her school, transforming a prison-like library (it even had bars!) into a vibrant learning commons. Mary Evangeliste interviewed Valerie in December of 2012.

Mary: We're impressed with and interested in the way you frame and communicate change in your organization. It's been about five years since you became a learning commons, correct?

Valerie: Yes, we started the transition to that name in the fall of 2008. We had an official grand opening on December 5, 2008, and at that time we really started to call it the "learning commons." But a lot of the library's programmatic work was "learning commons" style for many years.

Mary: So as you went through that process, and especially the planning, were you thinking about how you were talking about and framing change, or were you just doing it? How you were talking with teachers and students and administrators?

Valerie: The bottom line was getting more students into the space in a more productive way. My main goal was to change the space so that it was a place where students felt comfortable, a place that students respected, so that kind of change had to come with reorienting and training staff. We need to make students feel welcome, give them tools where they would feel productive and be more academically successful. Slowly we started to change the landscape and the culture of the space. By rearranging it and making it more comfortable, and by not posting rules and jumping on students the moment we thought they did something wrong, but by showing some mutual respect, well, I found that really helped even some of my worst customers. All of this happened not in a conscious way, but it was really based on making students feel more comfortable, more respected and more successful academically, more creative in touching base with different departments.

Mary: So it has been some time since you became a learning commons. How do you think all these changes impacted your overall library operations?

Valerie: It's huge. The changes that we've made have made students more respectful of the space. They also really like coming there to learn because we don't post rules. We let kids talk, and we have spaces that allow them to sit in groups or to work in groups. Whether it's with paper and pen and books, or whether it's with technology, we encourage them to come in. We have comfortable seating that we let them put their feet on, because it doesn't matter. We have tried to create an atmosphere of collaboration, of group work, of creativity. We have fewer rules and more freethinking. Students say I think that it has made a huge difference in how our space is used by both teachers and students.

Mary: What about your instructional activities and your collaborations with your faculty and your teachers?

Valerie: Well, I continue to do the traditional kinds of things. I mean there are still some teachers who want that. Books for school projects—that has not gone away. But I also do other things. For instance, I'm working with students in the Science department who are doing a debate on global warming. Part of what I do guides these students through that information maze as we have done for many years. So I do the very traditional library work with classes. But we also incorporate a lot of different types of communication tools, web tools from Prezi to Animoto to Glogster. We work with students from setting up accounts to teaching them how to use the different tools to communicate what it is they want to show their peers and their teachers. We also set up the opportunity for students to comment on their peers' work, which the students find really helpful and exciting. They get to see what everyone else is doing online and they get to make constructive comments about their fellow classmates' work.

Mary: When you first became the school librarian at the high school did you think about how you were going to talk with the teachers or did you just go ahead and start doing it? Did you have any background in developing communications strategies?

Valerie: Well, I worked as an elementary school librarian for many years and then prior to that I was a classroom teacher. I was never a high school teacher, but I did know that we needed to change some of what we were doing, so I just sort of jumped in with both feet. I probably made a lot of mistakes, but I did try to get teachers to trust me, and that took time. I tell my Simmons students that it takes two to three years, sometimes four years, to get to know teachers well enough to establish a relationship. It takes time to get teachers to trust you as a valued resource, someone who is capable of working with their students. Teachers become very protective of their classrooms. I don't know if I had a plan, I just knew that we needed to get more students in the library more constructively. So I just approached the different departments and went to the department meetings; all the typical things all school librarians do. I also tried to incorporate the new and the different. I was pulling teachers away from doing the traditional essay and encouraging them to use different tools with their students and they were thrilled with that.

Mary: So, would you say that when you're talking to your students at Simmons, you advise them to be tenacious in their relationships with teachers?

Valerie: Oh, absolutely tenacious, and to be realistic. Not every teacher is going to jump on board. One of the biggest things is don't get stuck staying in your space, don't think that people have to always come to you. You go to them, and when teachers see you making that effort, they're also more willing to get on board. It could be a new teacher that comes in really needs extra help, or it could be an older teacher who is bogged down and needs some help getting students more engaged. You have to do that process diplomatically.

Mary: Now that the space is redone, how do you continue to communicate change within your organization?

Valerie: We get to talk to all the students at the beginning of their careers in high school, and I think that is a very good thing. I also think trying to keep on the cutting edge of things is important. Continually showing the new and different, showcasing that to students and staff. We are ordering what we call

Apple TV so that we can have students connect wirelessly to a sixty-inch flat panel screen on the wall. Each device has an opportunity to take over the screen so that students can work collaboratively and they can showcase what they're doing. I think that's important.

Mary: So when you have something new like that, how do you communicate that to staff and stakeholders?

Valerie: I make sure I write everything into an annual report. I make a report that is very interactive and post it online so that it's easy to read and easy to go through. Every Friday the principal puts out what he calls a weekly blast and in that I have a column where I highlight and showcase new things. I have a Learning Commons listserv-type of thing where I send out messages. We constantly have events and performances in the Learning Commons and I send out notifications of those things, as well as more academic notifications. I also have a Twitter feed. I tweet out to the community about libraries and digital learning and e-books and readers and all kinds of different things. So those are just some of the ways that we reach out to our staff and students.

Mary: And what would you say to your students at Simmons if they said, "well that seems like a lot of work after you've already done X." Let's say, for example, you were talking about the Apple TV. Communicating about a new service is a whole other job that starts after you've done the "real" work.

Valerie: Yes, it's some extra effort, but first of all, delegate if you can. If you are one person in a school library, with no staff, that makes things very difficult. But if you are in a high school, you can enlist the help of students. I find that students are extremely tech savvy and many of them are very, very willing to jump in and be helpers. We have a whole group of students that helps me manage my iPads. We actually met with the Technology Director and she was so impressed with their level of enthusiasm and dedication to the project that she gave them all the passwords and let them upload apps to me and purchase apps from my volume-purchasing site. Yes, initially it seems insurmountable, but it's not. For instance, setting up a Twitter feed. Initially it might take you ten minutes to get an account going and to name it but tweeting things out to the community is seconds long, that's all. That's an important means of communication. Sending out a little newsletter blurb out at the end of the week or whatever ... when an idea comes across, just jot it down. You can manage your time to get these things to work, and you can delegate whether you have a staff or don't have a staff, somehow there is a way to find some extra help so that you're not doing it all alone.

Mary: We read an article by Paul Mihailidis, and you told him that even years after, sometimes parents will comment, saying students should be learning more in the library, not just playing instruments and drinking coffee. When you hear something like that how do you respond? What would you say to that person?

Valerie: If they're high school students and they're on a fully scheduled day, they need a place to go to have some downtime and to actually know that there are people in the school that they can ask questions of, that they have a caring space, a safe space. Much of what I do is all about that, and if parents would say well "why is all I hear about is coffee and music performances," then I would actually show them more about what we do. But I would also say to them, look, every experience is a learning experience, and if I get students into the Learning Commons by offering a coffee hour or by having a performance at lunch time, that only makes them more comfortable about me and about the space. Then they'll be comfortable seeing us when they really have an academic need, so it all intertwines. Learning is all about a variety of things. We've been doing listening lunches for I think twelve years now, and it's really grown and we have students who are graduated from college who will often mention those experiences as one of the highlights of their high school career.

Mary: Wonderful!

Valerie: In January, we have what we call an Alumni Listening Lunch, and the college students and beyond will come back and perform for the high school. We have some of our initial, first-time performers who will come back year after year because they were so devoted to this whole thing. What better way to get kids to say that libraries aren't boring places, they're places where they like to come. If we can get them in the door for any reason, then they'll come in the door for academic reasons as well.

Mary: Exactly, it's all about a comfort level.

Valerie: Absolutely. It's about a comfort level, and developing a culture of community. What we're really talking about in the Learning Commons is a community center, that's my philosophy.

Mary: Excellent. How do you feel that you keep up for yourself and for your staff; how do you keep the momentum and the enthusiasm up?

Valerie: I think about that all the time. Am I getting stale? Am I getting old? I'm probably two to three years from retiring. I've been doing this a long time.

I have six grandchildren now and a seventh on the way. So I think about that a lot. One of the things that keeps me from getting stale is being involved in all my local and national organizations. And I always encourage my students or anyone who's in the library field to be involved. Because when you attend conferences, or even attend them virtually, you're hearing from other school librarians and talking about new things and new ideas. I'm the president of the Massachusetts School Library Association, I'm on the executive board and I go to conferences. I got my school to agree to give me that opportunity to go. Unfortunately, not everybody has that freedom.

Mary: Excellent. Valerie, is there anything else you would want to communicate to the readers and to the students who are coming up after us?

Valerie: I think what's important about change is that not everyone is going to be on board right away. I was very lucky to work with an administration that respected me and trusted what I was doing. I think that working hard and getting your administrators to trust and respect you is huge because once you earn people's trust and respect, after that change becomes more natural. People will say, "She knows what she's doing or he knows what he's doing and let's give it a try." I think that's so important and that all dovetails into the leadership skills business. I'm hoping that new librarians have the leadership skills necessary to go into a school and convince other people that they are truly leaders. As school librarians, we are positioned to see what happens in the whole school, and that is a very unique position. You're not in a classroom working with just a set number of students every day, or maybe seeing other members of your department. Librarians are in a position to touch everyone's lives academically, professionally, and culturally and that is a very big role to play. So a message to other school librarians would be to realize the power you have, use it productively. Get on a couple of committees, be part of the faculty. Work with your accreditation groups and be a leader in the accreditation process, especially in secondary schools. All those things really help students, and staff particularly, see you as someone who is of value to the school as a whole.

Mary: This has been so helpful to us. I cannot thank you enough!

Case Study 8 | Rosenberg Library

AND THEN CAME the flood.

Some days it's hard to get out of bed and face the problems in our work-places. Budget issues, personnel conflicts, leaking roofs, and frustrating patrons—they can all conspire to make going to work a difficult task. But the next time you have the urge to hit the snooze button and crawl back under the covers, remember Maurine Sweeney's case study of Rosenberg Library in Galveston, Texas. Odds are, your day isn't going to be so bad after all.

Sweeney's case study is one of the most inspiring worst-case scenarios we've encountered. In 2008, the library faced dealing with the double whammy of Hurricane Ike and the global recession. Even in the midst of the disaster, library management took the time to think through processes using a planned abandonment lens, focusing on retaining services and practices that had the most local value, and abandoning or changing things that could be let go. We can all learn from these tough Texans and their ability to use the tools at hand to address a very real disaster.

After Ike

Evaluating Long-Held Practices under Scrutiny

Maurine Sweeney

ON SEPTEMBER 13, 2008, Hurricane Ike made landfall near Galveston, Texas, devastating the city and wiping out the first floor of the Rosenberg Library, one of the state's oldest public libraries. Facing major reconstruction expenses, a sudden, dramatic reduction in available collections and services, widespread devastation on the island and the prospect for reduced funding, the library was forced to lay off over half of its staff.

What library services to keep? What things to abandon? While the library had to move quickly, there was still the opportunity to thoughtfully respond and ensure that mission-critical services were saved, even as every single department in the library came under scrutiny. The Technical Services department went from four full-time equivalent staff in August of 2008 to one and a 0.5 FTE after the hurricane. Ordering, cataloging, and processing functions were consolidated into one full-time position.

It wasn't just staffing levels that were changing. As library management looked ahead, it was apparent that materials processing and copy-cataloging would need to be outsourced to handle the workload. Ordering was consolidated through a handful of vendors that were vetted for the level of customization they could provide, their cost estimate, and whether they supported EDI (electronic data interchange) ordering. Some of these changes were technical, exploiting technology to make the most efficient workflows. But the most compelling changes were philosophical, as long-held practices were questioned and evaluated. If something was no longer essential to the library's mission and its service to the Galveston community, it needed to be examined for possible abandonment. This case study will review the changes that made all the difference in preserving local value in a public library technical services unit.

Rosenberg Library: Background

Successor to the 1871 Galveston Mercantile Library, the Rosenberg Library is the oldest continuously operating public library in the state of Texas.[1] The building, constructed with funds donated by benefactor Henry Rosenberg, opened in 1904. Since its inception, the organization has been much more than a public library. The Galveston and Texas History Center houses one of the top four collections in the state of archival materials related to Galveston and Texas history. In addition to the archives, the library has a notable museum collection.

Galveston has a population of 47,743, down from 57,247 in 2000.[2] Annual library circulation is 251,372. The total number of active cardholders is 16,067. Prior to the hurricane, the Technical Services department consisted of a full-time clerk, cataloger, department manager and two part-time staff. In the fiscal year prior to the hurricane, the library added 14,720 physical items to the collection, the highest number on record. By comparison, the number of items received for the fiscal year 2008–2009 was 6,766, less than half. From October 2010 to October 2011, acquisitions activity was back up to 14,079 items with less than half the previous staff.

Evaluating Technical Services

In reality, the hurricane added urgency to addressing known issues. Inefficiencies within the Technical Services department had been evident prior to the storm; it took weeks for new orders to reach the shelves as they bottlenecked in the Cataloging department. The library director previously noted that there was room to improve the department's efficiency, and after the hurricane two key areas were identified for outsourcing: physical processing and procuring catalog records. Purchasing full MARC records from vendors was a considerable time-saver compared with locating, evaluating, and downloading records from subscription to cooperative catalogs. At $1.00 per record or less, the cost was considerably lower than the costs associated with hiring a full-time cataloger.

In addition, vendors could provide the materials and labor for physical processing: machine- and eye-readable barcodes, date and property stamps, date-due RF security tags, Mylar covers, A/V cases and artwork, and they could take advantage of economies of scale that our library could not. When the library had one full-time position that could essentially be devoted to processing new materials, it was more economical for those functions to be handled in-house. As that person's role took on many new dimensions, including acquisitions, receiving, and copy-cataloging, their time became too valuable to devote to a primarily clerical task. In the process of evaluating technical services, every aspect of the workflow—from placing an order for a book to the time that book gets to the shelf—would be changed.

Acquisitions: Identifying Problems, Crafting Solutions

PLACING ORDERS WITH A BOOK VENDOR

Without a strong technical services presence after the hurricane, some of the responsibilities for ordering books and communicating with vendors were spread out among selectors. The workflow was disjointed; selectors placed orders directly with the vendor, usually online. The content of these orders was printed and delivered to the acquisitions clerk who would then download brief "on order" records for the items in the cart. These brief records were either available for download through the vendor's website or full MARC records were copied and downloaded from shared catalogs.

Once the brief records were downloaded, a purchase order (PO) would be created in the Integrated Library System (ILS). The clerk would do a title search to locate the brief and/or existing bibliographic records. If a title search turned up an existing record, the brief record would be deleted or merged with the existing bib record and then added to the PO. Each PO line required certain data elements before it could be approved; once approved, the ILS would generate an item record allowing library patrons to place holds. A typical order might contain over a hundred PO lines and require an hour or more of work from start to finish. Something more efficient had to be developed.

The library's main vendor helped establish the use of 9XX tags for MARC records that include all the information necessary to automatically populate a purchase order and create a temporary item record. Many vendors offer these services, to varying degrees. Ultimately, the library chose to only continue vendor relationships with those that had compatible technology and services.

9XX tags are added to the MARC records provided by a vendor; a 970 tag is added to the MARC record with purchase order information, and a 949 tag is added with the information required for the system to generate an item record. Acquisitions import profiles are set up in the ILS to map the MARC tag data to the corresponding PO line data element. MARC import profiles used to import these records link to the corresponding acquisitions import map and use the match points determined by the administrator to either create new bib records or use existing records. If a match is found, the PO line is added without putting an additional bib record in the system and the item record is appended to an existing bib record.

Most of the vendors the library worked with were able to provide 9XX tags. One vendor could not provide 949 data, so the ILS import profile was manipulated to create a PO line item and item record off of the 970 tag. The ILS that this library uses does not accommodate batch changes to PO line fund codes, which presented challenges for staff. Alternatives to using vendor 9XX data include creating 9XX acquisitions data using software like MarcEdit or using batch edit functions in the ILS. The use of 9XX tags and the creation of corresponding ILS import profiles significantly streamlined the creation of purchase orders, eliminating hours of repetitive data entry.

Receiving and Paying for Orders

In a similar fashion, the old process for receiving materials and creating invoices was very time-consuming. Selectors submitted the orders but the acquisitions clerk generated the PO number the day that the order was created in the ILS. As such, the vendor did not have the correct PO number to put on the invoice that shipped with the materials. The clerk had to search the ILS to find what PO an item corresponded with so that it could be marked as received. To populate a statement, candidates for statement lines were identified by the ILS based on outstanding orders associated with a particular vendor. Each statement line had to be manually added with the units and extended price entered.

The use of electronic invoices is one of the key time-savers in the new process. EDI invoices are uploaded directly into the ILS and are immediately ready to be approved. At first, the time-saving benefits touted by the vendors sounded too good to be true. After talking with staff at several other libraries using EDI, it was apparent that those who had been using the system for a while were very satisfied. The librarians who took the time to explain how they set up EDI for their libraries and how it impacted their workflow were a persuasive testament to the efficiency of electronic ordering and invoicing.

Now, once the PO is created and approved, an EDI order is generated using a single button in the ILS and then submitted to the vendor's FTP site. The EDI orders capture the system control number for the bib record associated with a given PO line as well as the system control number for the temporary item records. This allows import profiles to be set up for the full or custom MARC records using the bib number as a match point and the item number as a match point, which enables a foolproof overlay point for incoming records. Once the order ships, the cataloger is delivered full MARC records by the vendor including 949 tags that overlay the brief "on order" records with completed item data such as barcode, call number, and collection. The library's ILS vendor and materials vendors were able to provide instructions for setting up EDI, which involved adding additional identifying data elements to vendor records in the ILS.

Cataloging

After the hurricane, the acquisitions clerk, who had received some training by the previous cataloger, assumed all copy-cataloging functions. She would go through the records for materials received and make edits to each record. Many of the edits were the same for multiple records, in particular deleting tags with vendor inventory data and adding the library's OCLC code to the 040 tag. Materials that required original cataloging or local call numbers were routed to the department manager.

ILS capabilities were identified that could make the copy-cataloging process more efficient. Different import profiles were set up for the various vendors that, depending on the match point, would either overlay or create a new record if there was not already an existing record. These import profiles could be set to batch delete particular fields upon import. In addition, Rosenberg employed MarcEdit, an open-source software tool, to make other batch changes to records that could not be addressed with the import profiles.

OUTSOURCING COPY-CATALOGING

When the library began outsourcing cataloging and processing, options with its main vendors were limited to two ends of a spectrum—either very customized records or generic records with library-specific holdings information. It was determined that the higher level of customization best suited the library's needs for the majority of books due to the number of existing records that had been created or edited by a professional cataloger. In addition, there were too many local practices to overhaul with the book collections, so it was essential to be able to communicate those site-specific details to the vendor. Costs per item vary with the level of service, from $1.99 per book for a full, unedited

MARC record and physical processing to just over $4.00 per item for fully customized cataloging, processing, and item data. A/V processing can range from $3–$5 depending on the item. This includes artwork, barcodes, security tags, property labels, and protective cases. In a year, the library can spend upwards of $30,000 for cataloging and processing—less than the costs for additional staff and materials.

The library's book vendor does a Z39.50 search of the catalog once an order has been submitted. They identify existing records and make a copy of those records to be sent back to the copy cataloger with the new 949 item tag once items are shipped. In this way, local edits are retained. The vendor also has a detailed file about how to catalog materials that are heavily collected, in particular local and state history and architecture, natural resources related to the area such as Gulf Coast birding guides, coastal plant life, fishing, and boating. The library's DVD collection is newer and did not have any special local cataloging rules. In turn, the library only purchases a generic MARC record from its A/V vendor. The same is true of the large-type, audiobook, and CD collections.

ADDED-VALUE CATALOGING

As librarians are able to leverage bibliographic data in new ways, it is of paramount importance that the efforts spent building important local or niche collections are not wasted due to incomplete or inaccurate data. While the library has outsourced most book cataloging, there are materials that require special consideration, in particular series for children and books for the library's archive, the Galveston and Texas History Center. Books purchased for the History Center are routed to the technical services manager for more extensive cataloging or to amend the record. Gifts of theses or self-published items often require original cataloging. Materials destined for the archives will remain in the collection in perpetuity, thus it is more important that the cataloging for these items be complete and accurate. Many records require contents or additional notes that highlight the local connection of the material. This added value is crucial for researchers.

When new children's books are received, the clerk routes items identified as children's series to the technical services manager. The clerk has received some training on series cataloging, in particular adding a 490 tag if it is not already in the record. From there, an 830 tag can be added by the cataloger. The series entries are only added to books; there are not adequate staff resources to trace series for all formats and the children's librarians more commonly received requests to locate books in a series within the catalog. The department has had positive feedback from the librarians about the ease of locating these items in the catalog now.

Staff Training

The way the technical services staff member orders and catalogs materials today is radically different from the process used before Hurricane Ike. The clerk who navigated all of these changes has worked at the Rosenberg Library for over 25 years. The library was very fortunate to have a staff member who, though dubious at first about the benefits of changing the system, quickly adapted to the new procedures and provided valuable input along the way. This institutional knowledge was incredibly useful. If she was not sure why a particular process or procedure was handled a certain way, then it meant the process was probably one that could be changed and she often championed changing long-held practices that no longer seemed relevant.

Striking the right balance between including staff in the process and not overwhelming them with details every step of the way is helpful for a smooth transition. As much as possible, new procedures were tested several times before documenting them and training the staff. It was also essential that the staff member keep track of problems as they arose and communicate them to their supervisor.

Library selectors had to be trained to apply "grid" (9XX) data on the vendor websites that were incorporated into templates for specific collections. Some vendor websites are more intuitive than others for applying this data.

For administrative training, resources were available through the ILS vendor, from the materials vendors themselves and from colleagues. A site visit was made to another library in the area that had implemented EDI and BISAC ordering. Though their library had a different ILS and did all of their processing and cataloging in-house, it was a useful demonstration of how electronic ordering and invoicing streamlined their processes and demonstrated some of the different workflow configurations available. The materials vendors were often willing to provide contact information for other libraries that had implemented EDI ordering. In addition, the instruction manual for the ILS proved an invaluable guide in setting up the system and identifying additional technical capabilities.

Communicating Changes to Library Staff and the Community

Changes to the library's acquisitions procedures have been highlighted in the library's annual report and annual meeting of the Board of Directors; of particular note were the efficiencies gained in terms of staff time and how quickly materials now reach the shelf, typically within one business day of receipt. The library has not publicized these changes to internal procedures but patrons do comment about how much faster new materials are available.

Moving Forward

Efforts to eliminate repetitive data entry and streamline collections and processes are ongoing. Library staff is encouraged to question why certain procedures are in place and whether they are still relevant. Within technical services, the acquisitions clerk has been able to help with additional projects: weeding, RFID tagging, providing copy-cataloging for special collections that had not previously been cataloged, and searching for misshelved items, to name a few. For the department manager, with less time required to assist with daily technical services tasks, efforts have shifted to database maintenance tasks and outsourcing authorities processing.

Hurricane Ike was absolutely devastating, and its floodwaters washed away much more than we will ever be able to imagine. But in its wake a new library culture of questioning and measured, planned abandonment has grown. Rosenberg Library has been tested, and is in a stronger position to face the future.

Bookend

GIVEN THE ROSENBERG Library staff's ability to focus on preserving local value in the midst of catastrophic stress, really the rest of us have no excuse. One of the key points in the case study is to optimize the ILS already owned by the library. By using tools at hand and resisting the urge to buy something shiny and new to solve a problem, librarians made the most of staff time and organizational resources. We all need to look at our technical services processes to determine just what provides the most local good, and how to be the best stewards of existing and aspirational institutional resources. Some libraries are moving forward with outsourcing, some are trying new web-based management services, and others are trying entirely new models of classifying and presenting materials to their communities through use of BISAC or other means. The pace of change in technical services is constant, and one of the areas where librarians have traditionally excelled in is embracing new technologies. The key, as Beth Thornton argues in her essay "The Existential Crisis of a Cataloger," is to "face the future while holding on to important aspects of the past."[3]

The work of technical services is to organize information to facilitate knowledge creation. By focusing on how our own communities use services, we can all make our cataloging tools and processes better, and perhaps free up valuable staff time and energy to create what R. David Lankes calls "collections of the community." Lankes states that "the most powerful arguments for libraries, aside from the brilliance of librarians, are around the theme of community platform for improvement and advancement."[4]

Rosenberg Library continues to focus on the community, and making smart choices to abandon—and to keep—what brings the most value to their stakeholders.

REFERENCES

1. Jane A. Kenamore, "ROSENBERG LIBRARY," *Handbook of Texas Online,* Texas State Historical Association, accessed July 27, 2012, www.tshaonline.org/handbook/online/articles/lcr02.

2. 2010 Census, 2000 Census.

3. Beth Thornton, "The Existential Crisis of a Cataloger, in Radical Cataloging: Essays at the Front, ed. K.R. Roberto, (Jefferson, NC: McFarland & Company, Inc., 2008) 13–17.

4. R. David Lankes, "Beyond the Bullet Points: Libraries are Obsolete," Virtual Dave . . . Real Blog, April 20, 2012, http://quartz.syr.edu/blog/?p = 1567&c page = 1#comment-4630.

Case Study 9 | # University of West Florida

IF YOU WANT to lead a visionary organization, you have to make the hard decisions first in order to give yourself the ability to move forward.

If, as David Lankes argues in his *The Atlas of New Librarianship,* the mission of librarians is to improve society through facilitating knowledge creation in their communities, then providing space for imagination, creativity, and inspiration is crucial to the future success of libraries. Librarians at the University of West Florida found their "great good space" by giving up artifacts that no longer served the needs of their communities (legacy print periodical collections) and transforming the space into a "third place" for conversation and learning, which leads to knowledge creation.

Getting people to mix, to converse, and to create knowledge isn't always easy and straightforward, and when dealing with legacy buildings, it can seem impossible. Librarians planning spaces rarely have the luxury of starting from the ground up, and reworking existing spaces can be a logistical nightmare. But creating other spaces for serendipitous collisions is crucial, as Melissa Finley Gonzalez and Amanda Westley Ziegler reveal in their case study.

The Great Good Place

Creating Space for Knowledge Creation

Melissa Finley Gonzalez and Amanda Westley Ziegler

IN SEPTEMBER 2010, the Dean of Libraries at the University of West Florida (UWF) charged a task force to review space in the John C. Pace Library and provide recommendations for improving the arrangement of patron areas, staff space, and collections. The eight-member task force conducted an exhaustive literature review, surveyed the university community, and visited other libraries in the Southeast (Florida State University, Tulane University, and Pensacola State College) that had recently completed renovation projects.

A number of common themes emerged during the literature review, including the need for comfortable furnishings, natural light, artwork and color, lower shelving, appropriate technology, and more collaborative group spaces and established quiet areas in the library. The task force developed an informal survey to seek input from patrons, populated with themes addressed in the literature. The survey was made available by placing it on a whiteboard near the elevators on the first floor of the library; cookies and questionnaires were placed at a table near the entrance of the library, survey boxes were installed in several locations in the library, library instruction classes were asked for feedback, an online survey was posted on the library web page, a pop-up survey followed the login process at library computers, and the administrators and directors of campus groups were e-mailed for dissemination among their constituents.

The survey simply asked patrons to mark "Yes," "No," or "Don't Care" by each item on the list, indicating their level of interest in having these items in their library. Space was provided for comments or additional suggestions, and we did not limit the number of times a patron could respond. We received 9,490 responses over a 16-day survey period. Over 50 percent of responses came from the online surveys, especially the pop-up survey that appeared during the login process. The whiteboard near the elevator was visible and proved to be a "low-tech" way of gauging public opinion, while the paper surveys were the least popular method. Overall, the results of the survey gave

FIG. 9.1

Survey Summaries

	Y	N	DC	TOTALS
More computers	744	41	43	828
Comfortable chairs	719	17	57	793
Group study rooms	675	29	66	770
Quiet area	668	27	35	730
Quiet floor	576	70	93	739
Writing center	569	65	75	709
Reading room	566	55	100	721
Big tables	482	86	124	692
Presentation rooms	469	62	174	705
Improve lighting	452	109	135	696
Peer tutoring	419	38	85	542
Art exhibits	362	50	252	664
Docking stations	356	119	126	601
Sofas	96	20	43	159
TV with news	41	58	11	110
Tables for 2	26	1	4	31
TOTALS	**7,220**	**847**	**1,423**	**9,490**

us a clear picture of our users' needs and expectations, and provided the following summary of statistics.[1] (See figure 9.1.)

More computers and comfortable chairs topped the list, while areas for group collaboration and quiet individual study and a reading room also ranked high on the list of desires. Fortunately, we were able to act on several of these items almost immediately. For example, we designated a quiet floor, installed more PCs and opened up our instruction room for computing when not reserved for classes, and added additional seating. Furthermore, plans to address group study spaces are currently underway.

As we considered the space on the library's second floor, we concluded that the Serials department staff did not need the 1,964 square feet of prime space they occupied. As a result of attrition and budget cuts, the Serials department had been reduced from six positions to two positions in less than five years. Two lines were cut, two were reassigned to other departments as part of a library-wide reorganization, and the two remaining Serials staff were ultimately folded into the Cataloging Services department on the first floor. This reorganization made sense because the UWF Libraries was receiving fewer and fewer print serials and no longer had the need for a traditional Serials department.

With the increased availability and continual addition of more and more online subscriptions, journal packages, and databases, most libraries have seen a steady decrease in print journal subscriptions, and UWF libraries is no exception. Furthermore, we just completed a lengthy and in-depth, focused review of individual subscriptions in order to increase access to electronic full-text content and maximize the purchasing power of the libraries' budget. The following chart illustrates the decline in print serials based on numbers from annual reports since 2001 (see figure 9.2).

Historically, the UWF Libraries calculated the number of subscriptions by simply taking the figure from the previous year's annual report and adjusting the total according to the number of serial titles added or cancelled during that next fiscal year. However, as part of the recent journal review project, we took an inventory of current print subscriptions and found the actual number to be much lower. This explains the drastic dip in 2011–2012.

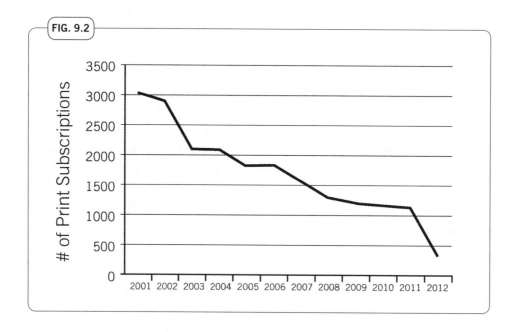

FIG. 9.2

Before the reorganization was implemented, we gradually reduced services offered by the Serials department on the second floor. We started by decreasing hours at the service desk, then closed the desk permanently while the staff were still physically there, before finally moving the staff to their new space on the first floor. This incremental reduction of services allowed us to assess the impact of closing down one of the library's public service points.

When we began decreasing hours at the Serials desk, we started with evening and weekend hours, which were lower traffic hours usually staffed by a student assistant. Signage referred patrons to the first floor service desks for assistance, and staff at the Information and Circulation desks tracked the number of questions received related to bound journals, microfilm, and second floor computer and printer issues. As part of this transition, all Reference and Circulation staff, including student assistants, received training on the microfilm readers and storage in order to adequately assist patrons. We also developed more comprehensive guides, available on the computers attached to our microfilm readers, to allow patrons to utilize the equipment with less staff involvement. When the decrease in hours caused only a small increase in the number of related questions asked at the Information and Circulation desks, Serials staff began leaving the desk "open" but unmanned during the weekday hours, eventually removing the bell from the desk, and then keeping the service window grates closed. Finally, after almost two semesters of a slow reduction in hours and services, the staff moved to their new space on the first floor.

The task force's original recommendation proposed turning the second floor space into a reading room. However, converting the entire fourth floor of the library into a quiet floor lessened the perceived need for a quiet reading room. Returning to the drawing board, two ideas emerged. The first was related to a university decision several years before to convert the main dining space on campus from an a la carte model with open seating to an all-you-care-to-eat buffet model. Thus, in order to sit in the area, you had to pay at the door. There was strong faculty opposition to the change based on the loss of space to mingle and converse with students and colleagues without needing to pay for a full meal or even bring a lunch.

The second idea was to look to the works of UWF Faculty Emeritus Dr. Ray Oldenburg for inspiration. Dr. Oldenburg is an urban sociologist and the originator of the idea of the "third space," or, as he refers to them in his works, the "Great Good Place." Dr. Oldenburg posits that there are three "realms of experience," the domestic, the gainful and productive, and the inclusively sociable, which must be balanced in order to have a relaxed and fulfilling daily life.[2]

With these two ideas in mind, it was clear that we wanted to move forward with a space that encouraged informal gathering and sharing amongst students and faculty. Thus, the Great Good Place was born.

In order to understand our goals for the space and the service that it provides to the university community, it is important to understand more about the idea of the Great Good Place. Oldenburg discusses the application of the third space on a college campus in this way:

> I suggest that learning takes place in three contexts. There is the classroom, where experts impart knowledge to novices and instruct them. There is private reflection: reading and reflection, writing and reflection, imagining and reflection... And there is conversation with others, especially with one's peers, but also with people who are different: younger, older, richer poorer, wilder, funnier, more political, less educated. It is often talk that is boisterous, noisy and heated.[3]

Using this concept, we began to plan a space that encouraged conversation and drew a wide variety of people. One of our main goals throughout the space study, and particularly in the conversion of the Great Good Place, was to emphasize the fact that libraries are not just physical locations for using resources and services—they can, and should, serve as spaces for intellectual discourse and scholarly collaboration. The John C. Pace Library, which is ideally situated in the center of the main campus, is particularly suited to this role.

The original space consisted of a large L-shaped central workspace, two smaller offices with doors that opened into the larger workspace, and two public service windows with counter workspace on the staff side and rolling grates for security when the desk was closed. The space had three entrances, including a service door near the freight elevator. Besides cosmetic changes to paint and carpet to brighten up the space, we made the decision to wall off the service entrance for both security and aesthetic reasons. We retained the openings for the public service desk, but removed the grates and installed plate glass windows in their place. This allows visual access to the space while keeping it (and the potentially noisy discussions we hoped would take place there) contained. We replaced the main entrance with a door with a large inset window, and kept the existing lighting fixtures throughout the space intact. The counters under the former public service windows were replaced with a counter of a similar height and depth that better matched the new colors in the room.

The innermost of the two former staff offices was converted into a room for vending machines and microwaves. As Oldenburg states, "Great hangouts are often connected with what Emerson called 'our institutions of daily necessity,' namely eating and drinking."[4] We hoped that the inclusion of the vending machines and microwaves, as well as the availability of snacks in the coffee shop on the library's first floor, would encourage eating and drinking within the space. The window looking out from the office to the main space was left in place, and the door was replaced with one with an inset window to increase the lines of sight into the room. The outer office was demolished to provide room for a faculty publications display case. The decision to include a built-in faculty publication case was an intentional strategy to encourage and foster communication between faculty members and students and to draw faculty into the space. The glassed-in upper portion of the case is lighted and holds works from faculty throughout the university, while open shelves in the lower half of the case hold issues of current newspapers and other popular periodicals.

Once decisions regarding the structure of the room were made, we began to investigate how best to utilize the large floor space in the middle of the room. The original proposal called for a fairly even ratio of tables to upholstered lounge, or "comfy," chairs. In developing the plan for furniture and organization of the space, the planning team solicited input from Dr. Oldenburg, who offered several recommendations for encouraging the use of the space for conversation and collaboration. He pointed out that round tables are more effective at facilitating conversation and also help to remove hierarchical distinctions—an important facet of the Great Good Place. In order for a place to truly function as a third space, "a transformation must occur as one passes through the portal of a third place. Worldly status claims must be checked at the door in order that all within may be equals."[5] We ordered sixteen tables of different heights, shapes, and sizes. The chairs were chosen for comfort, but also for their similarity to the types of seating and tables found in typical Great Good Places, such as coffeehouses or English clubs.[6] In addition to the tables, an L-shaped counter near the entrance provides seating for another six individuals. Four upholstered lounge chairs (only 5 percent of the total seats available in the space) are grouped around a low table. Dr. Oldenburg advised that these chairs have a low back and open sides to increase lines of sight and facilitate conversation.

Signage throughout the space encourages people to remember that the Great Good Place is a space for conversation and camaraderie and that quiet study areas are available on the fourth floor. We strive to encourage people to carry on normal-voiced conversations and to use the space for its intended purpose—collaboration and connection—without having to worry about disturbing others.

As for wall décor, we wanted more than wall color to provide visual inspiration for conversation. We installed a Walker Display system, a museum-quality art display solution that uses acrylic rods to hang artwork. Just as the faculty display case showcases faculty talent, the artwork in the Great Good Place is an opportunity to showcase the work and talent of our students. The Dean of Libraries made an adjustment to the job description of an existing library staff member with a background in art to account for liaison duties with the UWF art gallery manager and overseeing the rotation of student art in the Great Good Place and other display spaces throughout the library. The intention is to rotate out different art displays at least once per semester and to eventually serve as an alternative gallery space for final projects and other student exhibitions. By coordinating with the gallery director and the Art department, the UWF Libraries is able to take advantage of an already existing pool of art submissions, as well as an established set of policies and procedures. In addition to the student artwork, we utilized the American Library Association's READ software to create READ posters of faculty from throughout the university to place on the remaining columns and other wall spaces. These posters have proven to be immensely popular with both faculty and students.

Finally, to decorate the large plate glass windows that replaced the original service openings, we commissioned a haiku from Dr. Oldenburg and had it screened for the windows. It reads:

> Here we can gather
> Mid the circle of friendship
> And learn all the more

This sentiment not only pays tribute to the idea of the Great Good Place and the author of both the haiku and the Great Good Place concept, but it provides visual interest from outside the space, serves as an advertisement to draw people in, and clarifies the purpose of the space.

Another issue that arose during the planning period was the question of technology. While the Great Good Place has excellent wireless access and numerous existing Ethernet ports and electrical outlets, it is not intended as a space for technology. The UWF Libraries had recently renovated the fifth floor to create the SkyLab, a high-tech student learning space that offers a multitude of hardware, software, and other technological applications. Furthermore, as the survey indicated, students were not enthusiastic about TVs at the library. These factors supported Dr. Oldenburg's strong sense that technology often serves to inhibit conversation and face-to-face connection. Since it was our intention to foster communication and discourse, we purposefully avoided the inclusion of additional technology in the space. Patrons can (and do!) bring their laptops and mobile devices into the Great Good Place for various uses, but there is no fixed technology present in the room.

The Great Good Place opened in August 2011, and has become an extremely popular library destination. We held a grand opening celebration, where Dr. Oldenburg provided a brief presentation of his work and the "third space" concept. Employees from throughout the university who were familiar with the space before the renovation have expressed amazement at the transformation and have given a wealth of positive feedback about the space. Students and faculty alike have expressed their gratitude that the UWF Libraries was able to convert the space for use by the entire university community.

As with any popular space on campus, we quickly began to get requests to reserve the Great Good Place for various functions. However, since the purpose is to provide a common, public space, we have purposefully limited "reservations" to events that are open to the public and benefit from participation by a widespread segment of the campus population. The library has other spaces that are reservable for limited types of use by contacting the Administrative Assistant for the Libraries, so there has been no significant reaction to the limiting of reservations for the Great Good Place, nor was there a need to create any new policies or procedures.

Since its opening, the Great Good Place has hosted a number of events that encourage conversations and collaborations. It has been used for graduate student receptions, and a number of classes have held their end-of-semester poster sessions in the space, with valuable interaction from students and faculty both inside and outside of the class or discipline. Most recently, the UWF Women's Studies Program held a series of brown bag luncheons with various speakers from across campus for Women's History Month. Beyond these types of formal, scheduled events that are cleared in advance and coordinated with library staff, we have seen several inventive uses for the space. In addition to the faculty/faculty and student/faculty interactions we had hoped to see, we have seen university administrators use the space as a common ground with both faculty and students. The Dean of the College of Arts and Sciences, the largest college on campus, frequently holds open office hours for students and/or faculty in the Great Good Place. All of these events, both formal and informal, are usually advertised to the wider university community, but have been enhanced by the interaction with the passersby and other "random" members of the university community—exactly the types of interactions we had hoped to foster!

A comparison of statistics from year to year to demonstrate the decline of interactions at the Serials service desk is difficult to determine due to differences in the granularity of the statistics collected, but even with rough equivalents, a clear picture emerges. During the 2007–2008 fiscal year, when the first staff vacancy went unfilled in Serials, the Serials service desk saw an average of 112 requests per week. The following year saw a slight increase to 122 transactions per week, the majority of which were directional questions or referrals to other service points. In 2009–2010, the average number of weekly transactions took a sharp dive to 91. During this year, distinction was made for the first time between in-person, phone, and reshelving transactions, which had previously been lumped together. Of the average 91 weekly transactions, 60 were in person. Over half of these were directional or referrals. The last few months that the service desk was open, the number of transactions plummeted to 26 per week.

Conversely, recent head counts of the Great Good Place every 3 hours reveal that on an average week, 220 people can be found using the space. Despite the imprecise nature of head counting a space that is not equipped with a door counter, it is clear that the space is utilized far more as a gathering space than it was as a service point for the Serials department. Overall, the finished design of the space has been a hit with students, faculty, and staff, and head counts and feedback from users indicates that the repurposing of this space has been incredibly successful. As we envisioned, it has truly become a "great good place to meet, talk and linger."[7]

Bookend

RECENT LIBRARY BUILDING controversies, such as the disputes over design choices at the New York Public Library and the closure of library branches in Great Britain, remind us that space matters to everyone—and that the library as place is of paramount importance. Whether renovating an existing space or designing a new library, mindful planning at the start of a building project is key.

When Steve Jobs was designing the offices for Pixar Studios on the grounds of a former Del Monte plant in Emeryville, California, the original architectural design called for three separate functional buildings. Designers, engineers, and executives would be housed in separate offices. Jobs scrapped that plan, instead opting for one big, open, airy space, with the central purpose of enhancing collaboration. Jobs reportedly tweaked all aspects of the building's design, from mailboxes to bathrooms, with an eye to bringing people together in a serendipitous fashion. While following Steve Jobs' design choices at Pixar, where he purposefully centralized the location of bathrooms to ensure that staff from all divisions were brought together, might not be a realistic, the idea of fostering consilience through building design was brought to life at the University of West Florida. As libraries strive to become centers of knowledge creation, space becomes increasingly vital to the success of our endeavors.

REFERENCES

1. Space Study Task Force, "Building Program," John C. Pace Library, University of West Florida, accessed March 17, 2012, http://lgdata.s3-website-us-east-1 .amazonaws.com/docs/1663/268644/TF-space-usage-Building-Program.pdf.

2. Ray Oldenburg, *The Great Good Place: Cafés, Coffee Shops, Community Centers, Beauty Parlors, General Stores, Bars, Hangouts and How They Get You through the Day* (New York: Paragon House, 1989), 14–15.

3. Ray Oldenburg, "Making College a Great Place to Talk," in *The Best of Planning for Higher Education: An Anthology of Articles from the Premier Journal in Higher Education Planning*, ed. George Keller (Ann Arbor, MI: Society for College and University Planning, 1997), 90–91, accessed March 22, 2012, www.eric.ed.gov/ PDFS/ED472314.pdf.

4. Ibid., 93.

5. Oldenburg, *The Great Good Place*, 25.

6. Ibid., 24.

7. Oldenburg, "Making College a Great Place to Talk," 93.

Conclusion

"Before building or equipment or books, the librarian stands supreme.
The librarian is the center of the system and all else depends upon her."

— Arthur H. Chamberlain of the University of California,
in an address to the American Library Association, 1911

WHY DO WE fret so much about change? Do we see libraries as a static organism or a constantly changing idea? Buildings are built and get old, journals are no longer paper but delivered electronically, and we save materials in paper, microform, and digital formats. The demographics of our audiences change constantly. Chamberlain's quote could be from today, but instead it is from a speech given over one hundred years ago, and, in many ways, the same challenges that perplex us today have always perplexed librarians. If we take the long view, the historical view, we know that libraries are always transforming, and librarians are at the center of the transformation. If we accept that we are the center of the system, then we must also accept responsibility for whether the system works or is in need of repair. Librarians need to be the ones who do the ongoing maintenance, and we need to recognize that we will not be going back to some fabled golden age of libraries. There was, in all likelihood, no golden age of libraries. Among the many things we need to abandon is the nostalgia that unfortunately gives us an inaccurate perception of the past and hinders discussions of the present, and the future of libraries. That isn't to say, however, that we cannot learn from the past and be inspired by what has gone before. In the conclusion of his historical survey *Libraries and the Enlightenment,* Wayne Bivens-Tatum passionately argues that "in our beginning is our end." Librarians need, Bivens-Tatum argues, to return to the

Enlightenment ideals that founded and inspired our profession, and protect them for future generations.[1] In the same way, our call is to use our core values as the template for assessing our future services. Just as there was no "golden age" of libraries, there was no "golden age" of library services. Everything needs and deserves to be examined.

Planned abandonment is a vital and sane part of that ongoing upkeep and examination. Our lives would be more manageable if every time we add something, we at least consider taking something away. There is symmetry in this thinking. Giving up a service or a resource is not something that can be done without careful planning, thoughtful communication, and excellent leadership.

Librarians must understand that our libraries are not a static entity but a constantly evolving concept influenced by a variety of external and internal pressures. Our libraries will not always be a warehouse of books, a bank of computers, or [insert your own sentimental idea of libraries here]. Librarianship is not centered around a particular set of tasks but a particular way of thinking and this approach can lead us clearly into the future without fear. Librarians are trained to be critical thinkers; we analyze and make judgments and assessments in our daily work. From the case studies in this book, we can see examples of librarians who used their critical thinking skills to let go of something that was no longer needed. Some-

> "Libraries are keepers of knowledge and facilitators of literacy that enable the public to engage in a democratic society."
> —*R. David Lankes*

times this abandonment is initiated by external events—a flood, a hurricane, an extreme downturn in the budget. Sometimes it is initiated by internal events such as a change in leadership, a new technology to be harnessed, or a focus on a new demographic served. Sometimes the change can come swiftly and sometimes it can be incremental and gradual. This conclusion will summarize the main concepts that arose for us while working with our contributors who so honestly told their stories of planned abandonment. As always, there are lessons and there are aspirations. If we keep these ideas in mind, there will be no reason to fear our future and we can work to abandon fear—in ourselves and in our organizations.

We must move away from the idea that we are the keepers of books or that we are the keepers of any one kind of resource. This concept demands that we constantly challenge our assumptions about how a library collects, stores, and curates knowledge. Knowledge is a constant, but the delivery of it, and the means of facilitation will always change. The creation of knowledge is often tied to changes in technology and we must examine our prejudices to make sure we are not limiting ourselves and our ability to help our patrons. Just as our society and technology changes, so should we. The case study from Lafayette College is a great example. They challenged their own assumptions about buying subscription databases and instead moved to pay-per-view articles and ended up saving their organization a lot of money while providing broader and better access for patrons.

> "Contemporary libraries have shifted from warehouses of books and materials to becoming participatory sites of culture that invite, ignite and sustain conversations."
> —New York Times *article titled "Do we really need libraries?" on Dec 27, 2012, by Buffy Hamilton*

Now that we are no longer tethered to being a gigantic warehouse of books and print periodicals, what will we make of the space? Only ten years ago or so we were engaged in a debate concerning transitioning our print subscriptions to online databases. No more print journals to collect and preserve. At the time, this was a large hurdle but we overcame it and now Lafayette has taken the next step in that process by replacing print subscriptions with pay-per-view articles.

In the case study for the University of West Florida, we see a similar thread. They replaced their browsing periodicals and reference desk and opened up an amazing "third place." In this space, all types of people from campus meet, convene, and work on projects together. This third place certainly places this library in the center of knowledge creation and discourse at their university. As we transition from print to virtual resources, the physicality of our libraries has renewed importance.

Library As Space Takes on New Urgency

Libraries have never served one type of person. In public libraries, we develop and deliver programs for toddlers, teenagers, and all the way to mature populations. We develop our collections in relationship to our changing populations. In academic libraries, we serve all disciplines from the humanities through the hard sciences. We develop instruction for the first-generation student to the faculty member. We continue to redesign our spaces in accordance to these diverse populations. Accommodating all of these various needs and wants is challenging, but it is also one of our greatest strengths. As librarians, we are uniquely situated to create neutral, safe, and creative environments for all of our communities. In his article "The Library as Prototype of Cultural Diversity," sociologist Robert Ibarra states that libraries, and especially public libraries, have created or improved spaces in relation to the diverse communities they serve for over twenty-five years. They strive to serve various socio-economic groups, different genders, various races, religions, and languages. Cultural diversity seeks to understand the diverse ways different peoples communicate, learn, build relationships, and make decisions. He celebrates libraries as the place where context diversity can thrive. He defines context diversity as "a new paradigm that is systemic, inclusive, multidimensional. . . . It encourages reframing, rather than reforming . . . cultures to meet the needs of all populations. . . . Context diversity strives to create a learning community replete with myriad ways to attract diverse populations and have them thrive in an academic or workplace environment."[2] We can spend our time being sentimental over the demise of printed books or we can repurpose that space to open up possibilities like the University of West Florida did. As sociologist Ray Oldenburg explains in *The Great Good Place,* in order for an area to serve as a "third space," "a transformation must occur as one passes through the portal of a third place. Worldly status claims must be checked at the door in order that all within may be equals." Library as Space takes on new significance because we are not just a warehouse of books but a neutral, safe place where collaboration and creation are employed and enjoyed by all. This space can serve as an unbiased, inclusive, and secure space for all types of learners.

Communication—You Can Never Have Enough

When all library staff feel that they have participated in the dialogue, change will be more sustainable. This can be a particular challenge in libraries where studies have shown that traditionally we tend to be more introverted.[3] In the case study from American University Library, we see an innovative use of clickers to gather input anonymously from staff about ongoing changes. This technique would be useful in many libraries where reticent staff members may not always feel like equal participants in driving change. The richer the internal dialogue is about change within your organization, the less you will have to revisit your decisions.

Data is also a key element of communication, and the intelligent use of data was the backbone of American University and the Cumberland County Library's case study. Dave Consiglio's interview reminds us that in order to truly understand what's going on in your library, you need both qualitative and quantitative data. The best research, and the best management decisions, comes from both kinds of data, and in using that data to build a compelling narrative regarding change. Whether changing a technical services workflow, the management of a library website, or entire reference operation, as was the case with Oregon State University's case study, data and clear communication are key.

Once you have that narrative, you need to equally communicate inside and outside your organization about change. Not only is it important to clearly communicate to staff, peers, and directors about the ongoing service analysis, but it is also essential, once you have reached an internal decision to abandon a service, to communicate with all of your users. In the University of California, Santa Cruz (UC Santa Cruz) and the University of North Carolina at Charlotte (UNC Charlotte) case studies, we see that these libraries used a variety of ways to communicate the change. Will the users care? Will a small minority be unhappy? Very few of us will face the kind of backlash that occurred at the UC Santa Cruz Libraries when they limited their hours, but we can nonetheless learn from their experience. Be bold even if a vocal minority is upset by your decision to abandon—just keep communicating why. Users live in the same constantly evolving world that we live in; they know that everything is shifting. It is our responsibility to explain to them how libraries are responding and transforming also.

We must communicate why over and over again. There are two accepted principles in marketing that should be applied when abandoning a service. The first is just when you are getting sick of what you're communicating, the audience is finally getting the message. You are not your target audience. You and your target audience are different. So what may be old news to you and your staff still needs to be communicated externally to everyone else. Librarians and staff should use every available communication tool to announce the change in service. The second principle is that people need to hear something seven times before they retain the message. We live in an unprecedented time where we are bombarded by messages. Most of us feel cognitively overloaded. Your message about change is one of a thousand your user will receive in a day. It is essential to over communicate with your user when you abandon a service.

In addition to communicating successfully inside and outside our local organizations, we must also expand the way we communicate within our profession in general. We must share our challenges and successes equally. Sharing our successes is only half of the story. Many times at library conferences and through publications we only hear about good outcomes. There is no doubt that we should seek to inspire each other with innovation and success, but we must also share our challenges in order to learn and grow from one another. At an ALA Annual event in Anaheim, California, in 2008, Mary attended the MARS Chair's Program "What is the Future of Face-to-Face Reference?" and heard librarian Char Booth discuss her experience of introducing video reference service at Ohio University. Ms. Booth explained what a failure the new service was and gave specific and hilarious examples of why it did not work. Mary remembers feeling relieved that finally someone at a conference was honestly talking about why something did not work. It is just as important to present and write about initiatives and projects that don't work as well as the ones that are successful. Our case study contributors were also candid, not only telling us what works but also what did not work and what they would do differently in the future. Sharing our stories, regardless of the outcome, is the fastest way for us to map the uncertain future together.

We Have to Think about How We Think

In our library science graduate programs, we are explicitly taught to remain neutral during the reference interviewing process. We are taught to think critically and ask questions that unearth the users' needs through a series of probing questions. We are to conduct this interview the same whether the user is looking for statistics on infant mortality in a developing nation, child abuse in the USA, or strategies for arid desert gardening. As the ALA Code of Ethics explains, "We distinguish between our personal convictions and professional duties and do not allow our personal beliefs to interfere with fair representation of the aims of our institutions or the provision of access to their information resources."[4]

So how can we strive to bring this same type of dispassionate critical thinking to our own internal processes? Incorporating planned abandonment processes requires us to think critically about our own resources and services. It demands that we step away from personal emotion and sentimentality when examining legacy services. The answer cannot be, "This is how it's always been done," because that response does not fit within a critical construct.

Once we bring the same, unbiased point of view to our internal discussions as we do to our reference interviews, we will more rationally see what needs to stay and what needs to go.

That means we must think about how we think. Ask yourself: What biases are we bringing to the table? What emotions are impeding us? What rigid idea of "a library" is keeping us from seeing opportunities? We can go even further than that—what ideas are being brought to the table? What innovations are not being entertained? What solutions never see the light of day? We can begin to answer these questions through examining our business model: How do we create, develop, and deliver value to our users? Each library will answer these questions differently.

If our business model is outdated or too rigid, we may miss opportunities in the same way that Xerox did with personal copiers and with Ethernet. In the article "Business Model Innovation: Opportunities and Barriers," professor of business Henry Chesbrough points out that we must move beyond entertaining new technologies and viewing these emerging technologies through our existing business models, to examining the business models themselves. In the case of Xerox, which was focused on large industrial copiers and printers, many great ideas were orphaned.[5] Because Xerox could not see these ideas making money within their current structure, they were farmed out and developed by smaller, more nimble firms to great success. Specifically, Xerox missed their opportunity to capitalize on the personal printer market.

We are uniquely positioned, because of our dedication and adherence to critical thinking methods, to think critically about how we do business. We must bring critical thinking into our meetings and our processes. There could be no profession more able to do this than ours.

Further Fostering of Leadership and Diversity Is a Necessity

In order for planned abandonment to be anything more than a flashy management idea borrowed from the business community, we must continue to work diligently on creating skilled and brave leaders across all levels of our libraries and dedicate our profession to recruiting and harnessing a diverse work staff. These two ideas are paramount to the success of libraries in general and to adopting a systematic planned abandonment process in particular.

Leadership is a term with complex meaning. In their article "Library Leadership 2.0: Leading from Throughout the Library Organization," Downing, Rivera, and Winston state that, "leadership [is] about the management of meaning and narrative within a given context (library department, organization, community, or campus) to influence an outcome or set of outcomes, while empowering others to do the same."[6] This definition resonates for many reasons. It addresses the idea that a leader has to drive the communication process of planned abandonment from beginning to end. While that is happening, a leader shares the agency of decision making with his or her staff. When authority is shared across the organization, it inspires others to be involved, dedicated collaborators. A model of shared leadership contributes to an organization that understands why certain services are being abandoned. The staff in this type of organization can clearly communicate change to users.

There is no question that we need to diversify our workforce. The outcome of diversity counts shows a 1 percent gain from 2000 to 2009/2010 in the amount of ethnic and minority accredited librarians.[7] We also lack diversity in the types of personalities that are attracted to library work.[8] How does this lack of diversity in our workplace affect systematic analyses such as planned abandonment? In his book, *The Difference: How the Power of Diversity Creates Better Groups, Firms, Schools and Societies*, economist and political scientist Scott Page shows through case studies and mathematical models that diverse groups find solutions faster. Page says, "If we have people with diverse tools, they'll get stuck in different places. One person can do their best, and then someone else can come in and improve on it. There's a lot of empirical data to show that diverse cities are more productive, diverse boards of directors make better decisions, the most innovative companies are diverse."[9] Ideally, planned abandonment requires diversity of talent and perspectives. We must build on each other's knowledge bases. No one person will be a master of all of the skills and proficiencies required for librarianship. We need to acknowledge each other's strengths and weaknesses while building a stronger collaborative whole.

As a profession, we must continue to dedicate ourselves locally and nationally to develop leaders at all levels of the organization and value and harness diverse people and talent. There is no doubt that if we dedicate ourselves to these two priorities, we will have a dynamic, innovative, and energized workplace ready to map the future, whatever and wherever it may be.

REFERENCES

1. Wayne Bivens-Tatum, *Libraries and the Enlightenment*, (Los Angeles, CA: Library Juice Press, 2012), 186.

2. Roberto A. Ibarra, "A Place to Belong: The Library as Prototype for Context Diversity" in *Currents and Convergence: Navigating the Rivers of Change: Proceedings of the Twelfth National Conference of the Association of College and Research Libraries April 7–10, 2005, Minneapolis, Minnesota.* (Chicago: American Library Association, 2005), 3.

3. Mary Jane Scherdin and Anne K. Beaubien, "Shattering Our Stereotype: Librarian's New Image," *Library Journal* 120, no. 12 (1995): 35–38.

4. ALA Code of Ethics, www.ala.org/advocacy/proethics/codeofethics/codeethics.

5. Henry Chesbrough, "Business Model Innovation: Opportunities and Barriers." *Long Range Planning* 43, no. 2 (2010): 354–363.

6. Karen Downing, Alexandra Rivera and Mark Winston. "Library Leadership 2.0: Leading From Throughout the Library Organization." Bowker Annual (2012).

7. American Library Association, "Diversity Counts," www.ala.org/offices/diversity/diversitycounts/divcounts.

8. Mary Jane Scherdin and Anne K. Beaubien, "Shattering Our Stereotype: Librarian's New Image," *Library Journal* 120, no. 12 (1995): 35–38.

9. Claudia Dreifus, "A Conversation with Scott E. Page: In Professor's Model, Diversity = Productivity," *New York Times*, January 8, 2008, accessed March 16, 2013, www.nytimes.com/2008/01/08/science/08conv.html?_r=0.

About the Authors
and Contributors

MARY EVANGELISTE is the owner of Fearless Future, a marketing and design company that works primarily with nonprofits. She is the coauthor of the best-selling ALA title *Bite-Sized Marketing: Realistic Solutions for the Overworked Librarian*. Before devoting herself full-time to Fearless Future, Mary worked for over 20 years in libraries and museums. She has held positions at the Corcoran Gallery of Art, the Smithsonian, the National Gallery of Art, the American University Library, and the University of Arizona Libraries. Mary currently serves on the advisory board of First Book-Tucson and resides in Tucson, Arizona.

KATHERINE FURLONG was Director, Access and Technical Services at Lafayette College, where she also served as Project Manager for Lafayette's $22 million expansion and renovation of Skillman Library. Katherine has participated in the Frye Leadership Institute (2011), the ACRL/Harvard Leadership Institute (2006), and the Institute for Information Literacy. She has written and presented extensively on library administration, management, and instruction. She has served as president of the Delaware Valley chapter of the ACRL and is presently the president of the board of the Pennsylvania Interlibrary Delivery Service. In July 2014, Katherine transitioned to Susquehanna University, where she is the University Librarian/Director of the Blough-Weis Library.

CAROLYN BLATCHLEY is Training Services Coordinator for the Cumberland County Library System in Carlisle, Pennsylvania. Carolyn's previous experience includes working as the Director of Field Services for the Hemlock Girl Scout Council.

GREG CAREAGA is Head of Research, Outreach and Instruction at UC Santa Cruz, his alma mater. Before that he was Head of Teaching and Learning Services from 2009–2011, and Media Development Librarian from 2000–2009.

M. ELIZABETH COWELL is the Associate University Librarian for Public Services at UC Santa Cruz beginning in July 2008. From 2004–2008 she was the U.S. Government Information Librarian/Coordinator for Public and Technical Services for the Social Sciences Research Center at Stanford University and prior to that the Head of Data, Government and Geographic Information Services at UC San Diego.

ANNE C. ELGUINDI is currently Associate Director of the Virtual Library of Virginia (VIVA), the consortium of nonprofit academic libraries within the Commonwealth of Virginia. She holds a Master's Degree in Library Science from the University of North Carolina at Chapel Hill, and a Master's Degree in Statistics from American University.

MELISSA F. GONZALEZ is the Head of Reference at the John C. Pace Library at the University of West Florida. She holds a Master of Library and Information Science Degree and a Master of Arts in History Degree from the University of Southern Mississippi.

MICHAEL HANSON is the Director of Technical Services at Pima County Community College in Tucson, Arizona. From 2006–2013, he worked in a variety of professional positions at Lafayette College in Easton, Pennsylvania.

TERESE HEIDENWOLF is Director for Research & Instructional Services at Lafayette College Library in Easton, Pennsylvania.

ROBYN HUFF-EIBL is the Team Leader for Access & Information Services at the University of Arizona Libraries. She has worked at the University of Arizona Libraries for the past 20 years, holding a variety of positions with several different teams.

BETTY LADNER is the Associate University Librarian for Collections, Access and Outreach Services at the J. Murrey Atkins Library at the University of North Carolina at Charlotte. She has been a member of the Library Faculty (Associate Professor) there for 12 years, where she also served as the Distance Education Librarian for several years.

NICOLE LAWSON served as Head of Access Services/Circulation and Reserves at the University of California, Santa Cruz from February 2008 through June 2011. She is currently Public Services Coordinator at Sonoma State University.

CHERYL MIDDLETON is Associate University Librarian for Learning and engagement for the Oregon State University Libraries Teaching & Engagement Department. An active member of ACRL for over 17 years with appointments ranging from committee member, former chair of the University Library Section, and mostly recently, an appointment to the ACRL Research Planning and Review Committee.

LISA T. NICKEL is Associate Dean of Research and Public Service at Earl Gregg Swem Library at the College of William and Mary, and Adjunct Associate Professor at the University of Maryland University College. She served as Head of Access Services at the J. Murrey Atkins Library at the University of North Carolina at Charlotte from 2010–2013.

LUCIA ORLANDO is Head of the Government Publications and Law Unit at the University of California, Santa Cruz, in the McHenry Library Reference Section. She manages state, federal, and local government documents. She served as the Head of Research Services from 2009–2011, and has been a librarian for Government Information since 2002.

MAURINE SWEENEY is Library Services Manager at University of Texas, Moody Medical Library in Galveston, Texas. She received her MLS from the University of Maryland, College Park.

SARAH TROY is the Head of User Services and resources sharing at the University of California, Santa Cruz, where she received her Bachelor's Degree. She has been in this position, or similar, since 2006.

JEANNE F. VOYLES earned her Master's Degree in Library Science from the University of Arizona. She is currently the Team Leader of the Delivery, Description, and Acquisition Team at the University of Arizona Library. Jeanne has been a member of all four major restructuring project teams in the library since 1993.

AMANDA WESTLEY ZIEGLER is the Head of Circulation at the John C. Pace Library at the University of West Florida. She holds a Master of Library and Information Science Degree from the University of North Texas.

Bibliography

Albrecht, Karl. *The Power of Minds at Work: Organizational Intelligence in Action.* New York: AMACON, 2003.

American Library Association. "Audience Response Systems: Beyond the Classroom." http://presentations.ala.org/index.php?title = Audience_Response _Systems:_Beyond_the_Classroom.

American Library Association. "Code of Ethics of the American Library Association." www.ala.org/advocacy/proethics/codeofethics/codeethics.

American Library Association. "Diversity Counts Tables, 2012." www.ala.org/ offices/sites/ala.org.offices/files/content/diversity/diversitycounts/ diversitycountstables2012.pdf.

Baker, Nicholson. *Double Fold: Libraries and the Assault on Paper.* 1st ed. New York: Random House, 2001.

Bittman, Mark. "'Give Me Butter! Always Butter!'" *New York Times Magazine.* April 22, 2012.

Bivens-Tatum, Wayne. "Libraries and the Commodification of Culture." http://blogs .princeton.edu/librarian/2012/02/libraries-and-the-commodification-of -culture.

———. *Libraries and the Enlightenment.* Los Angeles, CA: Library Juice Press, 2012.

Chesbrough, Henry. "Business Model Innovation: Opportunities and Barriers." *Long Range Planning* 43, no. 2 (2010): 354–363.

Collins, Bobbie L., Rosalind Tedford, and H. David Womack, "'Debating' the Merits of Clickers in an Academic Library." *North Carolina Libraries* (Spring/Summer 2008): 20–24.

Cox, Richard J. *Vandals in the Stacks?: A Response to Nicholson Baker's Assault on Libraries*. Westport, CT: Greenwood Press, 2002.

Dreifus, Claudia. "A Conversation with Scott E. Page: In Professor's Model, Diversity = Productivity." *New York Times*. January 8, 2008.

Drucker, Peter F. *The Essential Drucker: The Best of Sixty Years of Peter Drucker's Essential Writings on Management*. New York: Collins Business Essentials, 2008.

———. *Managing the Non-Profit Organization: Practices and Principles*. New York: Collins Business Essentials, 2005.

Drucker, Peter F., and Peter M. Senge. *Leading in a Time of Change: What it Will Take to Lead Tomorrow, Viewer's Workbook*. New York: Jossey-Bass, 2001.

Evangeliste, Mary, and Katherine Furlong. "When Interdependence Becomes Codependence: Knowing When and How to Let Go of Legacy Services." In Declaration of Interdependence: The Proceedings of the ACRL 2011 Conference, March 30–April 2, 2011, Philadelphia, PA, 2011.

Fitzpatrick, Kathleen. *Planned Obsolescence: Publishing, Technology, and the Future of the Academy*. New York: NYU Press, 2011.

Foster, Nancy Fried, and Susan Gibbons, eds. *Studying Students: The Undergraduate Research Project at the University of Rochester*. Chicago: Association of College and Research Libraries, 2007.

Gilstrap, Donald L. "Librarians and the Complexity of Individual and Organizational Change: Case Study Findings of an Emergent Research Library." *Advances in Library Administration and Organization* 28 (2009): 1–58.

Goodson, Kymberly Anne, and Linda Frederiksen. "E-Reserves in Transition: Exploring New Possibilities in E-Reserves Service Delivery." *Journal of Interlibrary Loan, Document Delivery & Electronic Reserve* 21, no. 1-2 (2011): 33–56.

Hammond, Carol. "Arizona Libraries: Books to Bytes." Contributed Papers Presented at the AzLA Annual Conference (Phoenix, Arizona, November 17–18, 1995).

Hoffman, Christina, and Susan Goodwin. "A Clicker for Your Thoughts: Technology for Active Learning." *New Library World* 107, no. 9/10 (2006): 422–433.

Hutson, Matthew. *The 7 Laws of Magical Thinking: How Irrational Beliefs Keep Us Happy, Healthy, and Sane*. New York: Hudson Street Press, 2012.

Ibarra, Roberto A. "A Place to Belong: The Library as Prototype for Context Diversity." In *Currents and Convergence: Navigating the Rivers of Change:*

Proceedings of the Twelfth National Conference of the Association of College and Research Libraries April 7–10, 2005, Minneapolis, Minnesota. Chicago: American Association of Libraries, 2005.

John C. Pace Library. "Building Program—John C. Pace Library." http://lgdata .s3-website-us-east-1.amazonaws.com/docs/1663/268644/TF-space -usage-Building-Program.pdf.

Kahneman, Daniel. *Thinking, Fast and Slow.* New York: Farrar, Straus and Giroux, 2011.

Lakos, Amos, and Shelley Phipps. "Creating a Culture of Assessment: A Catalyst for Organizational Change." *Portal: Libraries and the Academy* 4, no. 3 (2004): 345–361.

Lankes, R. David. *The Atlas of New Librarianship.* Cambridge, Mass.: MIT Press, 2011.

———. "Beyond the Bullet Points: Libraries are Obsolete." *Virtual Dave . . . Real Blog.* April 20, 2012. http://quartz.syr.edu/blog/?p = 1567&cpage = 1#comment-4630.

Lehrer, Jonah. *Imagine: How Creativity Works.* Boston: Houghton Mifflin Harcourt, 2012.

Lewis, David W. "Clay Shirky on Newspapers and What It Can Teach Academic Libraries." *Indiana Libraries* 31, no. 1 (2012): 54. http://journals.iupui .edu/index.php/IndianaLibraries/article/viewFile/2068/1947.

———. "A Strategy for Academic Libraries in the First Quarter of the 21st Century." *College & Research Libraries* 68, no. 5 (2007): 418–434.

Lukerson, Victor. "Girl Scouts use Social Media, Mobile Tech to Break Cookie Sales Records." *Time.com,* November 2, 2012. http://business.time.com/ 2012/11/02/girl-scouts-use-social-media-mobile-tech-to-break-cookie -sales-records.

Martell, Charles. "The Absent User: Physical Use of Academic Library Collections and Services Continues to Decline 1995–2006." *The Journal of Academic Librarianship* 34, no. 5 (2008): 400–407.

Massey-Burzio, Virginia. "Reference Encounters of a Different Kind: A Symposium." *Journal of Academic Librarianship* 18, no. 5 (1992): 276–280.

Mery, Yvonne, Rebecca Blakiston, Elizabeth Kline, Leslie Sult, and Michael Brewer. "Developing an Online Credit IL Course for a Freshman Writing Program in a University Setting." In *Best Practices for Credit-Bearing Information Literacy Courses.* Edited by Christopher V. Hollister. Chicago: Association of College & Research Libraries, 2010.

Nutefall, Jennifer E., and Faye A. Chadwell. "Preparing for the 21st Century: Academic Library Realignment." *New Library World* 113, no. 3/4 (2012): 162–173.

Oldenburg, Ray. *The Great Good Place: Cafés, Coffee Shops, Community Centers, Beauty Parlors, General Stores, Bars, Hangouts, and How They Get You Through the Day*. New York: Paragon House, 1989.

———. "Making College a Great Place to Talk," in *The Best of Planning for Higher Education*. Edited by George Keller. Ann Arbor, Michigan: Society for College and University Planning, 1997.

Pritchard, Sarah M. "Deconstructing the Library: Reconceptualizing Collections, Spaces and Services." *Journal of Library Administration* 48, no. 2 (2008): 219–233.

Ryan, Susan M. "Reference Transactions Analysis: The Cost-Effectiveness of Staffing a Traditional Academic Reference Desk." *The Journal of Academic Librarianship* 34, no. 5 (2008): 389–399.

Safian, Robert. "Letter from the Editor: The Adrien Brody Rule." *Fast Company* (February 2012): 11.

Scherdin, Mary Jane, and Anne K. Beaubien. "Shattering Our Stereotype: Librarian's New Image." *Library Journal* 120, no. 12 (1995): 35–38.

Shapiro, Fred. "Quotes Uncovered: Who Said No Crisis Should Go to Waste," *Freakonomics: The Hidden Side of Everything*. http://freakonomics. com/2009/08/13/quotes-uncovered-who-said-no-crisis-should-go -to-waste.

Shirky, Clay. "Newspapers and Thinking the Unthinkable." www.shirky.com/ weblog/2009/03/newspapers-and-thinking-the-unthinkable.

Stoffle, Carla J. and Cheryl Cuillier. "From Surviving to Thriving." *Journal of Library Administration* 51, no. 1 (2011): 130–155.

Stoffle, Carla J., Kim Leeder, and Gabrielle Sykes-Casavant. "Bridging the Gap: Wherever you are, the Library." *Journal of Library Administration* 48, no. 1 (2008): 3–30.

Strauss, William, and Neil Howe. *The Fourth Turning: An American Prophecy: What the Cycles of History Tell Us about American's Next Rendezvous with Destiny*. New York: Broadway, 1997.

Thornton, Beth. "The Existential Crisis of the Cataloger." In *Radical Cataloging: Essays at the Front*, edited by K. R. Roberto, 13–18. Jefferson, NC: McFarland, 2008.

University of Carolina. "About UNC Charlotte." www.uncc.edu/landing/about.

University of North Carolina. "Taxpayer Return on Investments (ROI) in Pennsylvania Public Libraries" Accessed July 25, 2013. www.ila.org/advocacy/ pdf/UNC_Pennsylvania.pdf.

Wayne, Richard. "The Academic Library Strategic Planning Puzzle: Putting the Pieces Together." *College & Research Libraries News* 72, no. 1 (2011): 12–15.

Wooldridge, Adrian. *Masters of Management: How the Business Gurus and Their Ideas Have Changed the World—for Better and for Worse*. 1 HarperCollins ed. New York: Harper Business, 2011.

Wu, Somaly Kim, and Donna Lanclos. "Re-Imagining the Users' Experience: An Ethnographic Approach to Web Usability and Space Design." *Reference Services Review* 39, no. 3 (2011): 369–389.

Zahra, Shaker A. "An Interview with Peter Drucker." *The Academy of Management Executive* 17, no. 3 (2003): 9–12.

Index

A

Academic Librarian blog, 29
access services, reorganizing and
  merging, 64–65
acquisitions
  placing orders with book vendors,
    114–115
  receiving and paying for orders,
    115–116
added-value cataloging, 117–118
administration, gaining trust and respect
  of, 109
Adrien Brody Rule, 1, 6
ALA Code of Ethics, 138
American University (case study). *See*
  strategic planning used to facilitate
  the shift to electronic resources
anthropological studies of student
  services (UNC Charlotte case study)
  article delivery, 78
  borrowing period, increasing, 78–79
  campus book delivery, changes to,
    77–78
  checkout period, increasing, 78–79
  collaboration with other library units,
    84

equipment, purchase and circulation
  of, 81–84
ethnographic research, 75–77
facilities use, 76–77
fines, elimination of, 79–80
interlibrary loans, 80–81
library anthropologist, working with,
  75–77, 84
overview, 73–75
public services, 77
ARIEL, 80–81
article delivery, 78
artwork, adding, 128
ASERL (Association of Southeastern
  Research Libraries), 81
The Atlas of New Librarianship (Lankes),
  121

B

Baker, Nicholson, 7
best practices for websites, 22
bias, moving beyond natural. *See* moving
  beyond natural bias to examine
  core services
Bivens-Tatum, Wayne, 29, 133
Blatchley, Carolyn, 14, 144

book delivery, changes to campus, 77–78
Booth, Char, 138
borrowing period, increasing, 78–79
branding goals, 23
"Bridging the Gap: Wherever you are, the
        Library" (Stoffle, Leeder, and Sykes-
        Casavant), xii, 37
Brody, Adrien, 1
budget cuts, moving to web-based services
        due to, 14–28
budget deadline, 61
business goals, 22–23
"Business Model Innovation: Opportunities
        and Barriers" (Chesbrough), 139

C
campus book delivery, changes to, 77–78
Careaga, Greg, 144
casual downloading of articles,
        incorporating a measure to prevent,
        3–4
cataloging
    added-value cataloging, 117–118
    outsourcing copy-cataloging, 116–117
    overview, 116
CCLS (case study). *See* moving to web-
        based services
chairs, adding comfortable, 127
Chamberlain, Arthur H., 133
change in libraries, 133–135
checkout period, increasing, 78–79
Chesbrough, Henry, 139
circulation stacks, integration of reference
        collection into, 46–48
CivicPlus Government Content
        Management System (GCMS), 17–18
clicker sets (student response systems),
        95, 136
collaboration with other library units, 84
collaborative strategic planning used
        to facilitate the shift to electronic
        resources. *See* strategic planning
        used to facilitate the shift to
        electronic resources
Collins, Bobbie L., 95
communication
    of changes to library staff and
        community, 119, 136–137

within the library profession, 138
    strategies for successful change,
        104–109
Consiglio, David, 8–12, 137
content management system (CMS), 26–27
context diversity, 136
conversation, creating a space that
        encourages, 126–128
core services, examination of. *See* moving
        beyond natural bias to examine core
        services
Cosby, Bill, 85
cost cutting and increasing access to
        periodicals, 2–7
Cowell, M. Elizabeth, 144
Cox, Richard, 7
critical services, reinventing. *See*
        reinventing critical services
critical thinking, 138–139
Cuillier, Cheryl, 88
cultural diversity, 136
Cumberland County Library System (case
        study). *See* moving to web-based
        services

D
data-driven approach to library
        management, 8–12, 137
delegating work, 107
delivery, changes to campus book, 77–78
design strategy for websites, 22–27
*The Difference: How the Power of Diversity
        Creates Better Groups, Firms, Schools
        and Societies* (Page), 140
Diggs, Valerie, 104–109
diversity, 136, 140
document delivery service, cutting, 62–63
*Double Fold: Libraries and the Assault on
        Paper* (Baker), 7
Downing, Karen, 139
downloading of articles, incorporating a
        measure to prevent casual, 3–4
Drucker, Peter, x, 37
Drupal, 18

E
eating and drinking, space for, 127
EBSCO Discovery Service, 80

editors for library websites, 19

electronic format, switching from paper journals to, 2–7

electronic invoices, 115–116

electronic reserve services, elimination of. *See* elimination of physical and electronic reserve services

electronic reserves, moving from paper reserves to, 32–33

electronic resources, strategic planning used to facilitate the shift to. *See* strategic planning used to facilitate the shift to electronic resources

Elguindi, Anne, 87, 102, 144

elimination of physical and electronic reserve services (University of Arizona at Tucson case study)

background information, 30–31

challenges in, 38–39

history of reserve process improvement, 31–34

lessons learned from, 38–40

moving from paper reserves to electronic reserves, 32–33

physical reserves, review and elimination of, 34–37

planned abandonment, 37–38

Emanuel, Rahm, 59

Emerald Strategies, 21–27

equipment, purchase and circulation of, 81–84

ethnographic research, 75–77

evaluation of long-held practices while under scrutiny (Rosenberg Library case study)

acquisitions

placing orders with book vendors, 114–115

receiving and paying for orders, 115–116

background information on Rosenberg Library, 113

cataloging

added-value cataloging, 117–118

outsourcing copy-cataloging, 116–117

overview, 116

communicating changes to library staff and community, 119

overview, 111–112

staff training, 118

technical services, evaluating, 113–114

Evangeliste, Mary, 104–109, 143

"The Existential Crisis of the Cataloger" (Thornton), 120

experiential data, 9–11

F

facilities use, 76–77

faculty opinion in the serials selection process, 4–6

federated library systems and creating and maintaining a website, 13–28

final reorganization, 68–71

fines, elimination of, 79–80

Fister, Barbara, 29

Fitzpatrick, Kathleen, 57

focus groups, 51–55

The Fourth Turning (Howe and Strauss), 72

"From Surviving to Thriving" (Stoffle and Cuillier), 88

FrontPage (Microsoft), 16

Furlong, Katherine, 8–12, 143

G

GCMS (Government Content Management System), 17–18

General Motors, xi

Gilstrap, Donald, xii

Girl Scouts Councils, xi, 13i

Gonzalez, Melissa Finley, 121, 144

Goodwin, Susan, 95

Granath, Kim, 95

"Great Good Place," 125–130

The Great Good Place (Oldenburg), 136

group study rooms, 70

H

Haivision, 36

Hanson, Michael, 144

Heidenwolf, Terese, 144

Hesselbein, Frances, x

Hoffman, Christina, 95

Horizon Information Portal (HIP), 26

hours, cutting, 63–64

Howe, Neil, 72
Huff-Eibl, Robyn, 29, 41, 144
Hurricane Ike, rebuilding of Rosenberg Library after. *See* evaluation of long-held practices while under scrutiny
Hutson, Matthew, 57

I

Ibaarro, Robert, 136
information and services to include on websites, 20
integration of the reference collections, 46–48
interlibrary loans, 80–81
invoices, electronic, 115–116

J

Jobs, Steve, 131
journal subscriptions, switching to pay-per-view periodicals from, 2–7

K

Kahneman, Daniel, 57, 58
knowledge creation, creating space for. *See* space review and creation

L

Ladner, Elizabeth, 73, 145
Lafayette College (case study), 1–7, 135
Lanclos, Donna, 75
Lankes, R. David, 120, 121
Lawson, Nicole, 145
leadership
    overview, 139–140
    turnover in, 60–61
"Leading in a Time of Change" (video), 37
learning commons, transforming a library into a, 104–105
learning management system (LMS), changing to a new, 67–68
Leeder, Kim, xii, 37
Lewis, David W., 86
LibQUAL+, 91
librarianship and change in libraries, 133–135
Libraries and the Enlightenment (Bivens-Tatum), 133

library activities, using website to promote, 26
library anthropologist, working with, 75–77, 84
"Library Leadership 2.0: Leading Throughout the Library Organization" (Downing, Rivera, and Winston), 139
Library Services and Technology Act (LSTA) grants, 18
library staff reduction, 65
"The Library as Prototype of Cultural Diversity" (Ibaarro), 136
Lukerson, Victor, 13

M

magical thinking, 57
MARC records, 9XX tags for, 114–115
MarcEdit, 115, 116
marketing precepts to apply when abandoning a service, 103, 137
McShae, Kathy, 21
Measure 42 (UCSC referendum to levy small fee on students to restore library hours for three years), 66
Medical Economics (Weiner), 59
Microsoft FrontPage, 16
Middleton, Cheryl, 43, 57, 145
Mihailidis, Paul, 108
Moodle, 77
move to a new, smaller building, 61
moving beyond natural bias to examine core services
    circulation stacks, integration of reference collection into, 46–48
    reference desk staffing
        background on OSU libraries, 44–46
        focus groups, 51–55
        integration of the reference collections, 46–48
        new reference service model, developing a, 48–51
    referral process, 55, 56
    subject expertise required for questions, method of handling, 50
    user satisfaction with reference desk services survey, 52

moving to web-based services
    (Cumberland County Library System
    case study)
    background on CCLS, 14–15
    history of CCLS web presence, 15–18
    methods used by CCLS to create
        and maintain a system-wide web
        presence, 19–20
    websites
        best practices, 22
        branding goals, 23
        business goals, 22–23
        creating, 21–22
        design strategy, 22–27
        information and services to
            include on, 20
        library activities, using website to
            promote, 26
        organizational culture, making
            website essential to, 26
        standards for, 25–26
        success measurements for, 25–26
        target users for, 23
        tasks, general website, 23–24
        technology constraints, 26–27
        usability of, 21–22, 23–25

N

natural bias, moving beyond. *See* moving
    beyond natural bias to examine core
    services
new reference service model, developing
    a, 48–51
"Newspapers and Thinking the
    Unthinkable" (Shirky), 85
Nickel, Lisa, 73, 145

O

Oldenburg, Ray, 125–126, 127, 128, 129,
    136
open holds, 35
open physical reserves, 35
Oregon State University (case study),
    43–58
organizational culture, making website
    essential to, 26
Orlando, Lucia, 145
outsourcing copy-cataloging, 116–117

P

Page, Scott, 140
paper reserves, moving to electronic
    reserves from, 32–33
participant observation, 73
pay-per-view periodicals, 2–7
paying for and receiving orders, 115–116
Pennsylvania Dynamic Site Framework
    (PA DSF), 16–17
physical reserve services, elimination
    of. *See* elimination of physical and
    electronic reserve services
physical reserves, review and elimination
    of, 34–37
Pixar Studios, 131
placing orders with book vendors,
    114–115
planned abandonment, x–xii , 37–38, 134
Point, Fernand, 28
print serials, decline in, 124
Pritchard, Sarah M., 88
profession, communication within the
    library, 138
Provocative Statements (Taiga Forum), 93
public services, 77

Q

qualitative data, 8–12
quantitative data, 8–12

R

"Re-imagining the users' experience: An
    ethnographic approach to web
    usability and space design" (Wu and
    Lanclos), 75
receiving and paying for orders, 115–116
redesign of library space, 135–136
reference desk staffing
    Oregon State University case study
        background on OSU libraries,
            44–46
        focus groups, 51–55
        integration of the reference
            collections, 46–48
        new reference service model,
            developing a, 48–51
    UCSC case study, 69
referral process, 55, 56

reinventing critical services (UCSC case study)
access services, reorganizing and merging, 64–65
budget cuts, 61
Collection Development department, 69
document delivery service, cutting, 62–63
final reorganization, 68–71
   group study rooms, 70
   hours, cutting, 63–64
   leadership, turnover in, 60–61
   learning management system (LMS), changing to a new, 67–68
   library staff reduction, 65
   Measure 42 (UCSC referendum to levy small fee on students to restore library hours for three years), 66
   move to a new, smaller building, 61
   overview, 60
   reference desk staffing, 69
   reorganization of department, 64
   Research, Instruction, Collections (RIC) model, 68
   Research, Outreach and Instruction (ROI), 69
   research services
      cutting, 63
      gathering data on, 66
      reorganizing, 65–66
   roving information student service, 71
   Shared Service Point Working Group (SSPWG), 67
   strategic planning, 61–62
   User Services and Resource sharing (US&RS), 70
reorganization of department, 64
Research, Instruction, Collections (RIC) model, 68
Research, Outreach and Instruction (ROI), 69
research services
   cutting, 63
   gathering data on, 66
   reorganizing, 65–66
Rivera, Alexandra, 139
Rosenberg Library (case study). *See* evaluation of long-held practices while under scrutiny

roving information student service, 71
Ryan, Susan, 49

S
Samson, Sue, 95
Schwarzenegger, Arnold, 61
Serials department, changes in, 123–125
The 7 Laws of Magical Thinking (Hutson), 57
Shapiro, Fred, 59
Shared Service Point Working Group (SSPWG), 67
Shirky, Clay, 85–86
Sykes-Casavant, Gabrielle, xii, 37
Slug Express, 62
smaller building, move to a, 61
space, redesign of library, 135–136
space review and creation (University of West Florida case study)
   artwork, adding, 128
   comfortable chairs, adding, 127
   conversation, creating a space that encourages, 126–128
   eating and drinking, space for, 127
   "Great Good Place," 125–130
   overview, 121–122, 135
   print serials, decline in, 124
   Serials department, changes in, 123–125
   survey of patrons, 122–123
   technology issues, 128–129
   wall decor, 128
staff
   reduction, 65
   training, 118
staff buy-in to the shift to electronic resources. *See* strategic planning used to facilitate the shift to electronic resources
standards for websites, 25–26
Stoffle, Carla J., xii, 37, 39, 88
strategic planning, 61–62
strategic planning used to facilitate the shift to electronic resources (American University case study)
   finalized actions, 100–101
   first planning session, 92–93
   future plans, 102

Information Delivery Services (IDS)
  defining, 89–90
  planning for IDS as part of
    university planning,
    90–91
  online discussions, 93–94
  outline for, 91–92
  overview, 88–89
  second planning session, 95–100
Strauss, William, 72
streaming media service, 36
student response systems (clicker sets),
    95, 136
subject expertise required for answering
    questions, 50
success measurements for websites, 25–26
survey of patrons, 122–123
Sweeney, Maurine, 111, 145

T

Taiga Forum, 93
target users for websites, 23
technical services, evaluating, 113–114
technology constraints, 26–27
technology issues, 128–129
Tedford, Rosalind, 95
Thinking, Fast and Slow (Kahneman), 57–58
The Thin Red Line (film), 1
Thornton, Beth, 120
transformation of libraries, 133–135
Troy, Sarah, 145

U

University of Arizona at Tucson (case
    study), 29–42
University of California at Santa Cruz
    (case study). *See* reinventing critical
    services
University of North Carolina at Charlotte
    (case study). *See* anthropological
    studies of student services

University of Rochester's Undergraduate
    Research Project, 73
University of West Florida (case study).
    See space review and creation
unpredictability in article use, statistics
    on, 4–6
usability of websites, 21–22, 23–25
user satisfaction with reference desk
    services survey, 52
User Services and Resource sharing
    (US&RS), 70

V

*Vandals in the Stacks? A Response to
    Nicholson Baker's Assault on Libraries*
    (Cox), 7
video reference service, 138
Voyles, Jeanne, 29, 41, 146

W

wall decor, 128
Wayne, Richard, 88
web-based services, moving to. *See*
    moving to web-based services
    (Cumberland County Library System
    case study)
Weiner, M. F., 59
Welch, Jack, xi
Wilder, Stanley, 75
Winston, Mark, 139
Womack, H. David, 95
Wu, Somaly Kim, 75

X

Xerox, 139

Y

Yale Book of Quotations (Shapiro), 59

Z

Ziegler, Amanda Westley, 121, 146